The Parenting Playbook: Strategies to Become Great Parents

Dhulia Bharat

Published by Dhulia Bharat, 2024.

THE PARENTING PLAYBOOK: STRATEGIES TO BECOME GREAT PARENTS

First edition. April 2, 2024.

ISBN: 979-8224791590

Written by Dhulia Bharat.

Table of Contents

Chapter 1: Introduction

- Overview of parenting

Parenting is a complex and multifaceted responsibility that involves the nurturing and upbringing of children from infancy through adulthood. It is a lifelong journey that requires patience, dedication, and a deep understanding of child development. Parents play a crucial role in shaping the physical, emotional, social, and cognitive development of their children, and are the primary influences in their lives.

One of the fundamental principles of parenting is fostering a loving and supportive relationship with your child. Research has shown that secure attachment between parent and child is essential for healthy emotional development. This involves providing consistent and sensitive care, responding to your child's needs, and creating a safe and nurturing environment. By building a strong bond with your child, you create a foundation of trust that will support their emotional well-being throughout their life.

Another important aspect of parenting is providing structure and guidance for your child. Setting clear boundaries and expectations helps children understand what is acceptable behavior and what is not. Consistent discipline is also key in teaching children to make responsible choices and learn from their mistakes. It is important for parents to strike a balance between being firm and being supportive, and to communicate expectations in a positive and constructive way.

Effective communication is essential in parenting, as it helps parents understand their child's needs, thoughts, and feelings, and allows children to express themselves and feel heard. Active listening, empathy, and open-ended questions are important tools for fostering positive communication with your child. By creating a supportive and non-judgmental environment, parents can encourage their children to share their experiences and concerns, and build a strong bond based on trust and respect.

Parenting also involves promoting your child's independence and autonomy. As children grow and develop, it is important to gradually increase their level of responsibility and decision-making authority. This helps children develop important life skills, such as problem-solving, decision-making, and self-regulation. By giving children opportunities to make their own choices and learn from their experiences, parents can empower them to become confident and capable individuals.

Parenting is not without its challenges. Every child is unique, with their own personality, temperament, and needs, and there is no one-size-fits-all approach to parenting. Parents must adapt their parenting style to meet the individual needs of each child, and be flexible and responsive to changing circumstances. From dealing with temper tantrums and power struggles to setting limits and managing conflicts, parenting requires patience, resilience, and a willingness to learn and grow. By fostering a loving and supportive relationship, providing structure and guidance, promoting independence and autonomy, and maintaining open and effective communication, parents can nurture their children's physical, emotional, social, and cognitive development, and help them grow into confident, capable, and well-adjusted individuals. While parenting comes with its challenges, the rewards far outweigh the struggles, and the bond between parent and child is a precious and enduring relationship that lasts a lifetime.

- Importance of parenting skills

Parenting skills play a crucial role in shaping the development and well-being of children. Along with providing love, guidance, and support, parents must also possess the necessary skills to navigate the challenges of raising a child in today's complex world. From setting boundaries and enforcing discipline to fostering emotional intelligence and cultivating healthy communication, parenting skills encompass a wide range of abilities that directly impact a child's overall growth and success.

One of the key reasons why parenting skills are important is their influence on a child's behavior and socialization. Parents serve as the primary role models for their children, shaping their attitudes, values, and beliefs through their own words and actions. By demonstrating positive behaviors, such as kindness, empathy, and responsibility, parents can instill these virtues in their children and help them develop into well-adjusted individuals who contribute positively to society. On the other hand, parents who lack essential parenting skills may unknowingly pass on negative patterns of behavior, leading to issues such as aggression, defiance, or social difficulties in their children.

In addition to behavior and socialization, parenting skills also play a significant role in promoting academic success and cognitive development in children. Parents who are actively involved in their child's education, provide a stimulating learning environment at home, and encourage curiosity and critical thinking can significantly enhance their child's academic performance and intellectual growth. Furthermore, effective communication and problem-solving skills taught by parents can help children develop strong analytical and decision-making abilities, which are essential for academic success and lifelong learning.

Moreover, parenting skills are crucial for fostering emotional intelligence and resilience in children. Emotional intelligence, or the ability to identify and manage one's own emotions as well as understand and empathize with others, is a vital skill that influences one's relationships, mental health, and overall well-being. Parents who possess strong emotional intelligence skills themselves can model healthy emotional expression and regulation to their children, helping them develop self-awareness, emotional control, and empathy towards others. By teaching children how to cope with stress, manage conflict, and build positive relationships, parents can equip them with the tools they need to navigate life's ups and downs with resilience and confidence.

Furthermore, parenting skills are essential for promoting positive communication and conflict resolution within the family. Effective communication skills, such as active listening, clear expression of thoughts and feelings, and respectful dialogue, are crucial for building strong parent-child relationships based on trust, understanding, and mutual respect. By fostering open and honest communication with their children, parents can create a supportive and nurturing environment where children feel safe to express themselves, seek guidance, and receive emotional support when needed. Moreover, teaching children constructive ways to resolve conflicts, negotiate differences, and communicate assertively can help them build healthy relationships with others and develop strong interpersonal skills that will benefit them throughout their lives. From behavior and socialization to academic achievement and emotional intelligence, the skills that parents possess have a profound impact on their children's development and future prospects. By cultivating positive parenting skills such as setting boundaries, fostering emotional intelligence, promoting academic success, and encouraging effective communication, parents can create a supportive and nurturing environment that nurtures their children's growth, resilience, and happiness. Ultimately, investing in parenting skills is an investment in the future of our children and society as a whole.

Chapter 2: Understanding Your Child

- Child development stages

Child development is a fascinating and complex process that involves a series of stages through which a child progresses from infancy to adulthood. These stages are characterized by distinct changes in physical, cognitive, emotional, and social development. Understanding these stages is essential for parents, educators, and healthcare professionals to provide appropriate support and guidance to children as they navigate their way through the various challenges and opportunities that come with each stage of development.

The first stage of child development is infancy, which typically lasts from birth to around 18 months of age. During this stage, infants experience rapid physical growth and development, as well as significant changes in their sensory and motor skills. Infants begin to explore and interact with their environment through touch, taste, sight, and sound, developing a sense of curiosity and wonder about the world around them. They also start to form attachments to their primary caregivers, usually their parents or other close family members, which lays the foundation for future relationships and social development.

The second stage of child development is early childhood, which begins around 18 months of age and extends to around 6 years of age. During this stage, children continue to grow physically and develop their motor skills, language abilities, and cognitive capabilities. They also begin to develop a sense of independence and autonomy, as well as a growing understanding of themselves and their place in the world. Early childhood is a critical period for social and emotional development, as children learn important social skills such as sharing, taking turns, and cooperating with others. They also start to form friendships and develop a sense of empathy and compassion for others.

The third stage of child development is middle childhood, which typically spans from 6 to 12 years of age. During this stage, children continue to grow physically and develop their cognitive and social skills further. They also start to develop a sense of self-identity and self-esteem, as well as a growing awareness of their own emotions and the emotions of others. Middle childhood is a time of significant cognitive growth, as children learn to think logically, solve problems, and understand complex concepts. They also start to develop a sense of morality and ethics, as well as an understanding of right and wrong.

The fourth stage of child development is adolescence, which begins around 12 years of age and extends to around 18 years of age. During this stage, adolescents experience rapid physical changes as they undergo puberty and develop secondary sexual characteristics. They also experience significant cognitive, emotional, and social changes, as they start to question authority, challenge established norms and values, and seek greater independence from their parents and other adults. Adolescence is a time of exploration and experimentation, as adolescents try to figure out who they are and what they believe in. It is also a time of heightened emotions and peer pressure, as adolescents navigate the complex social dynamics of their peer group and try to establish their own identity. Each stage is characterized by distinct changes in physical, cognitive, emotional, and social development, as children grow and learn to navigate the challenges and opportunities that come with each stage of development. Understanding these stages is essential for parents, educators, and healthcare professionals to provide appropriate support and guidance to children as they grow and develop. By recognizing and respecting the unique needs and abilities of children at each stage of development, we can help them reach their full potential and become healthy, happy, and well-adjusted adults.

- Communication with your child

Communication with your child is a crucial aspect of parenting that plays a significant role in their development and overall well-being. As parents, it is important to establish open and honest lines of communication with your child from a young age. By fostering a supportive and nurturing environment for communication, you are laying the foundation for a strong and healthy parent-child relationship.

One of the key elements of effective communication with your child is active listening. This involves not only hearing what your child is saying but also showing genuine interest in their thoughts, feelings, and experiences. By actively listening to your child, you are demonstrating that you value and respect their perspective, which in turn helps to build trust and strengthen your bond with them. Additionally, active listening allows you to better understand your child's needs and concerns, enabling you to provide the necessary support and guidance.

Another important aspect of communication with your child is the use of positive reinforcement. It is essential to praise and encourage your child for their efforts, achievements, and good behavior. By acknowledging and celebrating their successes, you are boosting their self-esteem and confidence, which are crucial for their emotional and social development. Positive reinforcement also helps to foster a positive and supportive relationship between you and your child, creating a nurturing and loving environment for them to thrive.

In addition to active listening and positive reinforcement, it is vital to communicate with your child in a clear, respectful, and age-appropriate manner. Avoid using negative language, criticism, or harsh tones when talking to your child, as this can have a detrimental impact on their self-esteem and overall well-being. Instead, focus on using encouraging and affirming language that motivates and inspires your child to be their best self. Remember to adjust your communication style and vocabulary based on your child's age and developmental stage, ensuring that your messages are easy to understand and resonate with them.

Furthermore, communication with your child should be a two-way street. Encourage your child to express their thoughts, feelings, and opinions openly and honestly, without fear of judgment or criticism. Create a safe and non-judgmental space for your child to share their concerns, fears, and joys with you, fostering a sense of trust and security in your relationship. By actively engaging in conversations with your child and seeking their input, you are empowering them to develop their communication skills and critical thinking abilities, which are essential for their growth and development.

It is also important to be patient and understanding when communicating with your child. Remember that they are still learning and growing, and may not always have the vocabulary or emotional intelligence to express themselves effectively. Be patient and supportive, and give your child the time and space they need to communicate their thoughts and feelings. Avoid interrupting or dismissing their concerns, and instead, listen attentively and respond empathetically to their needs. By showing compassion and understanding towards your child, you are fostering a healthy and nurturing environment for communication to flourish. By actively listening, using positive reinforcement, communicating respectfully and age-appropriately, fostering a two-way dialogue, being patient and understanding, you can create a supportive and nurturing environment for your child to thrive. Remember that communication is a continuous process that requires effort, empathy, and understanding from both parties. By prioritizing open and honest communication with your child, you are laying the groundwork for a strong and lasting parent-child relationship built on trust, respect, and love.

- Building a strong parent-child relationship

Building a strong parent-child relationship is crucial for the well-being and development of a child. Studies have shown that children who have a close and positive relationship with their parents are more likely to thrive academically, socially, and emotionally. This bond between parent and child serves as a foundation for the child's sense of security, self-esteem, and overall mental health. It is important for parents to cultivate this relationship from an early age, as the quality of the parent-child bond can have lasting effects on the child's future relationships and success in life.

One of the key factors in building a strong parent-child relationship is communication. Open and honest communication between parents and children is essential for establishing trust and understanding. It is important for parents to listen to their children and validate their feelings and experiences. By actively listening to their children, parents can gain insight into their child's thoughts, feelings, and needs. This can help parents better connect with their children and address any issues or conflicts that may arise. Communication also involves setting clear and consistent expectations for behavior, as well as providing constructive feedback and guidance.

Another important aspect of building a strong parent-child relationship is spending quality time together. Engaging in activities that both parent and child enjoy can help strengthen their bond and create lasting memories. Whether it's playing a board game, going for a walk in the park, or cooking a meal together, spending time together can foster a sense of connection and closeness. It is important for parents to be present and engaged during these activities, as it demonstrates to the child that they are valued and loved. Quality time together can also provide opportunities for parents and children to talk, laugh, and share experiences, further deepening their relationship.

Consistency and predictability are also key components of building a strong parent-child relationship. Children thrive on routine and knowing what to expect from their parents. By establishing consistent rules, boundaries, and expectations, parents can create a sense of stability and security for their children. Consistency also helps to build trust and reliability in the parent-child relationship. When parents are consistent in their discipline, praise, and support, children are more likely to feel secure and confident in their relationship with their parents. Predictability allows children to anticipate and understand their parent's reactions and behaviors, which can reduce anxiety and confusion.

Positive reinforcement is another important strategy for building a strong parent-child relationship. Acknowledging and praising children for their efforts, accomplishments, and positive behaviors can boost their self-esteem and confidence. Positive reinforcement can take many forms, such as verbal praise, hugs, high fives, or special privileges. It is important for parents to provide specific and genuine praise to their children, as this can help reinforce desired behaviors and strengthen the parent-child bond. By focusing on the positive aspects of a child's behavior and character, parents can help build a sense of self-worth and validation in their child.

Building a strong parent-child relationship takes time, effort, and patience. It is important for parents to prioritize their relationship with their children and make it a priority in their daily lives. By practicing open communication, spending quality time together, maintaining consistency and predictability, and providing positive reinforcement, parents can create a strong and supportive bond with their children. A strong parent-child relationship can have a lasting impact on a child's well-being and success, providing them with the foundation they need to thrive in all areas of their lives.

Chapter 3: Effective Discipline Techniques

- Setting guidelines and boundaries

Setting guidelines and boundaries is an essential aspect of maintaining order and efficiency in any organization or group setting. Whether it be in a workplace, classroom, community, or family, establishing clear expectations and boundaries helps to create a positive and productive environment for all involved. Guidelines and boundaries serve as a framework for behavior, decision-making, and interactions, ensuring that everyone is on the same page and working towards common goals.

One key reason for setting guidelines and boundaries is to establish standards of behavior and performance. By outlining what is expected of individuals in terms of their actions, attitudes, and work ethic, organizations can ensure that everyone is working towards the same objectives. This clarity helps to avoid confusion, conflicts, and misunderstandings, as everyone knows what is expected of them and what the consequences are for not meeting these expectations.

In addition to providing structure and guidance, setting guidelines and boundaries also helps to foster a sense of accountability and responsibility among individuals. When people know the boundaries within which they must operate, they are more likely to take ownership of their actions and take responsibility for their decisions. This can lead to increased motivation, productivity, and commitment to the organization's goals and values.

Furthermore, setting guidelines and boundaries can help to create a sense of safety and security within a group setting. By clearly defining what is and is not acceptable behavior, individuals can feel more confident in expressing themselves, sharing their ideas, and engaging with others. This can lead to better communication, collaboration, and trust among group members, which is essential for building strong relationships and achieving common objectives.

It is important to note that setting guidelines and boundaries should be done in a thoughtful and inclusive manner. It is not enough to simply dictate rules and expect everyone to comply without question. Instead, it is important to involve all stakeholders in the process of developing guidelines and boundaries, ensuring that their input is taken into consideration and that they understand the reasoning behind the rules that are being put in place.

When setting guidelines and boundaries, it is also important to be flexible and open to feedback. As circumstances change and new challenges arise, it may be necessary to adjust the guidelines and boundaries to better meet the needs of the organization or group. By remaining open to feedback and willing to adapt as needed, leaders can ensure that the guidelines and boundaries remain relevant and effective over time. By establishing clear expectations, standards of behavior, and boundaries, leaders can help to promote accountability, responsibility, and collaboration among individuals. By involving all stakeholders in the process and remaining open to feedback, guidelines and boundaries can be developed in a way that is inclusive, effective, and sustainable. Ultimately, by setting guidelines and boundaries, organizations can create a supportive and empowering environment that enables individuals to thrive and achieve their goals.

- Positive reinforcement

Positive reinforcement is a powerful tool in shaping behavior and promoting learning in individuals of all ages. It is a technique used in psychology and education to increase the likelihood that a desired behavior will be repeated by following it with a stimulus that is perceived as rewarding. This can include verbal praise, a pat on the back, a smile, or any other type of positive feedback that the individual finds motivating. Positive reinforcement is based on the principles of operant conditioning, a theory developed by psychologist B.F. Skinner in the 1930s. According to Skinner, behaviors that are positively reinforced are more likely to be repeated in the future, while behaviors that are not reinforced or punished are less likely to occur again.

Positive reinforcement can take many forms, depending on the individual's preferences and what they find rewarding. For some people, a simple "good job" or a thumbs-up gesture may be enough to reinforce a behavior, while others may require more tangible rewards such as a sticker, a treat, or a token that can be exchanged for a larger reward later on. The key is to find out what motivates the individual and tailor the reinforcement accordingly. It is important to note that positive reinforcement is not the same as bribery, as it is intended to encourage positive behavior rather than simply rewarding compliance.

One of the main benefits of using positive reinforcement is that it can help to build self-esteem and confidence in the individual. When a person receives positive feedback for their efforts and achievements, they are more likely to feel good about themselves and believe in their own abilities. This, in turn, can lead to increased motivation and a willingness to take on new challenges. Positive reinforcement can also help to strengthen relationships and build trust between individuals, as it fosters a sense of mutual respect and appreciation.

In addition to promoting positive behaviors, positive reinforcement can also be used to extinguish undesirable behaviors. By focusing on rewarding the behaviors that we want to see more of, we can effectively ignore or redirect behaviors that we want to discourage. This is known as the principle of extinction, and it can be a powerful tool in changing behavior over time. For example, if a child is constantly interrupting others during class, the teacher can use positive reinforcement to reward the child for raising their hand before speaking, while ignoring the interrupting behavior. Over time, the child will learn that raising their hand is the more effective and rewarding way to get attention, and the interrupting behavior will decrease.

Another important aspect of positive reinforcement is its role in shaping behavior through a process known as shaping. Shaping involves reinforcing successive approximations of a desired behavior until the final behavior is achieved. This can be particularly useful when working with individuals who are learning a new skill or behavior that is complex or difficult to achieve all at once. By breaking the behavior down into smaller, more achievable steps and reinforcing each step along the way, we can help the individual to build the necessary skills and confidence to reach their ultimate goal. This approach is often used in education, therapy, and other settings where behavior change is required.

It is important to note that positive reinforcement is most effective when it is delivered consistently and immediately following the desired behavior. The timing of the reinforcement is crucial, as the individual needs to be able to make a connection between their behavior and the reward in order for the reinforcement to be effective. If too much time elapses between the behavior and the reinforcement, the individual may not understand why they are being rewarded, which can weaken the association between the two. In addition, it is important to vary the types of reinforcement that are used, as individuals may become desensitized to a particular reward over time. By mixing up the rewards and keeping things interesting, we can maintain the individual's motivation and engagement in the behavior change process.

Positive reinforcement is a highly versatile and effective tool that can be used to promote learning, shape behavior, and build self-esteem in individuals of all ages. Whether in the classroom, at home, or in the workplace, positive reinforcement can help to create a positive and supportive environment that encourages growth and development. By understanding the principles of positive reinforcement and implementing them consistently, we can help individuals to reach their full potential and achieve success in their endeavors.

- Consistency in discipline

Consistency in discipline is a crucial aspect of maintaining order and promoting a positive learning environment in any setting, whether it be a classroom, workplace, or home. When rules and consequences are consistently enforced, individuals know what is expected of them and are more likely to adhere to the established guidelines. Inconsistent discipline can lead to confusion, resentment, and a lack of respect for authority figures. It is important for those in positions of leadership to be firm yet fair in their approach to discipline, setting clear expectations and consistently holding individuals accountable for their actions.

One of the key benefits of maintaining consistency in discipline is that it helps to instill a sense of fairness and equity among those being disciplined. When rules are applied inconsistently, individuals may feel as though they are being unfairly targeted or treated differently from their peers. This can lead to feelings of resentment and a lack of trust in authority figures. By consistently enforcing rules and consequences, individuals can see that everyone is held to the same standards and that decisions are not based on favoritism or bias.

Consistency in discipline also helps to establish a sense of predictability and stability in the learning environment. When individuals know what to expect in terms of rules and consequences, they are more likely to behave in a manner that is in line with those expectations. This can create a more harmonious and productive atmosphere, where individuals can focus on their tasks and responsibilities without the distraction of uncertain or arbitrary consequences.

Furthermore, consistency in discipline can help to promote accountability and responsibility among those being disciplined. When individuals know that they will face consequences for their actions, they are more likely to think twice before engaging in behavior that could result in disciplinary action. This can help to deter negative behavior and promote a culture of respect and responsibility within the group.

It is important for leaders to be approachable and friendly in their approach to discipline, while still maintaining a sense of professionalism and authority. Individuals are more likely to respond positively to discipline when it is delivered in a respectful and empathetic manner. It is important for leaders to listen to the concerns and perspectives of those being disciplined, and to be open to discussing potential solutions that are fair and reasonable. By maintaining clear expectations, enforcing rules and consequences consistently, and approaching discipline with a sense of fairness and empathy, leaders can help to create a culture of respect, responsibility, and accountability among those under their authority. It is important for leaders to actively engage with those being disciplined, listen to their perspectives, and work collaboratively to address any issues that arise. By prioritizing consistency in discipline, leaders can help to create a more harmonious and productive environment for all individuals involved.

Chapter 4: Building a Support System

- Importance of a support network

A support network is often defined as a group of individuals who provide emotional, practical, and sometimes financial assistance to one another. This concept is crucial in both personal and professional settings, as it plays a vital role in an individual's overall well-being and success. Having a strong support network can help individuals navigate challenges, cope with stress, and achieve their goals more effectively. Whether it is seeking advice, sharing resources, or simply having someone to listen, a support network can provide invaluable support and encouragement.

One of the key reasons why having a support network is important is that it can help individuals overcome obstacles and setbacks. Life is full of challenges, and having a group of people who can offer guidance, perspective, and encouragement can make a significant difference in one's ability to navigate difficult situations. When facing a personal crisis or professional setback, having a support network to lean on can provide a sense of comfort and reassurance. Knowing that there are people who care about you and are willing to help can give you the strength and resilience to persevere in the face of adversity.

Additionally, a support network can also play a critical role in helping individuals cope with stress. The demands of daily life, work, and relationships can often be overwhelming, leading to feelings of anxiety, isolation, and burnout. By having a support network in place, individuals can have a safe space to express their feelings, seek advice, and receive emotional support. This can help reduce feelings of loneliness and provide a sense of connection and belonging, which are essential for maintaining mental and emotional well-being.

Furthermore, a support network can also be instrumental in helping individuals achieve their goals and aspirations. Whether it is pursuing a new career path, starting a business, or embarking on a personal project, having a group of people who believe in you and support your endeavors can make a significant difference in your success. A support network can offer valuable insights, advice, and resources that can help you overcome obstacles, identify opportunities, and stay motivated and focused on your goals.

In addition to providing emotional and practical support, a support network can also offer social connections and networking opportunities. Building relationships with like-minded individuals who share similar interests, values, and goals can create a sense of camaraderie and community. These connections can open doors to new opportunities, partnerships, and collaborations that can benefit both your personal and professional growth. By expanding your social circle and building meaningful relationships, you can enhance your social capital and create a powerful network of contacts that can support and empower you in various aspects of your life. Whether it is seeking advice, sharing resources, or simply having someone to listen, a support network can provide the emotional, practical, and social support needed to thrive in today's fast-paced and increasingly complex world. By cultivating and nurturing strong relationships with a diverse group of individuals who believe in you and support your growth and success, you can create a strong foundation for personal and professional fulfillment. Remember, we all need a little help now and then, and having a support network in place can make all the difference in your journey toward a more fulfilling and successful life.

- Balancing work and family life

Balancing work and family life is a common challenge that many individuals face in today's fast-paced and demanding world. In our society, there is often an expectation to excel in both our careers and our personal lives, leading to feelings of overwhelm and stress as we try to juggle multiple responsibilities. However, with proper planning and prioritization, it is possible to find a healthy balance between work and family that allows for success in both areas.

One of the first steps in balancing work and family life is to establish clear boundaries between the two. It is important to recognize that work and family are two distinct aspects of our lives that require separate attention and care. By setting boundaries such as designated work hours and family time, individuals can create a sense of structure and organization that helps to prevent burnout and maintain a healthy work-life balance.

Another key aspect of balancing work and family life is effective time management. With so many responsibilities to juggle, it is essential to prioritize tasks and allocate time accordingly. This may involve creating a schedule or to-do list to help individuals stay on track and ensure that important tasks are completed in a timely manner. By managing time effectively, individuals can prevent feelings of overwhelm and ensure that they have time for both work and family commitments.

In addition to time management, communication is a crucial component of balancing work and family life. It is important to communicate openly and honestly with both employers and family members about expectations and priorities. By setting clear expectations and boundaries with employers, individuals can avoid overworking and ensure that they have time for their families. Similarly, open communication with family members can help to establish a sense of understanding and support when it comes to balancing work and family commitments.

Self-care is another important aspect of achieving a healthy work-life balance. Taking care of oneself is essential for maintaining overall well-being and preventing burnout. This may involve engaging in activities that promote relaxation and stress relief, such as exercise, meditation, or hobbies. By prioritizing self-care, individuals can recharge and rejuvenate, allowing them to be more present and engaged in both their work and family life.

Furthermore, flexibility is key when it comes to balancing work and family commitments. Life is unpredictable, and unexpected events or emergencies may arise that require adjustments to our schedules. By remaining flexible and adaptable, individuals can better navigate the demands of work and family life while also maintaining a sense of balance and harmony. It is important to remember that it is okay to ask for help or delegate tasks when needed, as no one can do it all alone.

Ultimately, balancing work and family life is a continual process that requires effort, patience, and dedication. By setting boundaries, managing time effectively, communicating openly, prioritizing self-care, and remaining flexible, individuals can achieve a healthy work-life balance that allows for success and fulfillment in both their professional and personal lives. It is important to remember that everyone's balance will look different, and what works for one person may not work for another. Finding the right balance that works for you and your family is a journey that requires reflection, self-awareness, and a willingness to make adjustments as needed.

- Seeking help when needed

Seeking help when needed is a crucial aspect of personal and professional development. Whether it is in the context of reaching out for emotional support, seeking academic assistance, or requesting guidance in the workplace, the ability to recognize when help is required and to take the necessary steps to obtain it is a sign of strength and self-awareness. However, some individuals may struggle with the notion of seeking help, viewing it as a sign of weakness or inadequacy. This perception is not only misguided but can also hinder one's growth and hinder their ability to achieve their goals. In this article, we will explore the importance of seeking help when needed, the benefits that come from doing so, and practical strategies for overcoming barriers to seeking assistance.

One of the key benefits of seeking help when needed is the opportunity to gain new perspectives and insights that can lead to personal growth and development. By consulting with others who have expertise or experience in a particular area, individuals can broaden their understanding of a given topic and learn new strategies for overcoming challenges. This can be particularly valuable in the academic setting, where students may feel overwhelmed by complex concepts or coursework. Seeking help from professors, tutors, or classmates can provide clarity and guidance that can help students succeed in their studies. Similarly, in the workplace, seeking help from colleagues or supervisors can lead to improved performance and career advancement.

Another important benefit of seeking help when needed is the opportunity to build meaningful relationships with others. By reaching out for assistance, individuals demonstrate vulnerability and a willingness to collaborate with others. This can foster a sense of trust and camaraderie that can lead to deeper connections and a supportive network of peers. In the academic setting, forming study groups or seeking guidance from mentors can create a sense of community and belonging that can enhance the learning experience. In the workplace, seeking help from colleagues can lead to stronger teamwork and collaboration, ultimately benefiting the organization as a whole.

Despite the many benefits of seeking help when needed, some individuals may struggle to do so due to various reasons. One common barrier to seeking help is the fear of judgment or criticism from others. Individuals may worry about appearing incompetent or needy, leading them to avoid reaching out for assistance even when it is clearly needed. This fear is often rooted in societal norms that equate asking for help with weakness or failure. However, it is important to recognize that seeking help is a sign of strength and self-awareness, not a sign of inadequacy. By reframing the narrative around seeking help, individuals can overcome this barrier and embrace the opportunities for growth and learning that come from reaching out to others.

Another common barrier to seeking help when needed is pride or ego. Some individuals may have a strong sense of independence and self-reliance, making it difficult for them to admit when they need assistance. This can stem from a desire to appear self-sufficient and in control at all times. However, it is important to recognize that no one can achieve success entirely on their own. Everyone needs help and support from others at some point in their lives. By acknowledging this fact and being willing to ask for help when needed, individuals can overcome this barrier and take advantage of the resources and expertise that others have to offer. By recognizing when assistance is required and taking the necessary steps to obtain it, individuals can gain new perspectives, build meaningful relationships, and overcome barriers to success. While there may be challenges and fears associated with seeking help, it is important to remember that asking for assistance is a sign of strength and self-awareness, not weakness. By reframing the narrative around seeking help and embracing the opportunities for growth and learning that come from reaching out to others, individuals can unlock their full potential and achieve their goals.

Chapter 5: Promoting Healthy Habits

- Nutrition and exercise for children

Proper nutrition and exercise are essential components of a healthy lifestyle for children. It is important for parents and caregivers to understand the importance of providing nutritious foods and encouraging physical activity to support children's growth and development. By developing healthy habits early on, children can establish a strong foundation for lifelong health and well-being. A well-balanced diet that includes a variety of fruits, vegetables, whole grains, lean proteins, and dairy products is key to meeting children's nutritional needs. It is important to limit the consumption of sugary beverages, processed foods, and high-fat snacks, as these can contribute to weight gain and other health issues.

Additionally, portion control is an important aspect of nutrition for children. It is important to provide children with appropriate portion sizes to help them maintain a healthy weight and avoid overeating. Parents and caregivers can use visual cues, such as using smaller plates and bowls, to help children understand proper portion sizes. Encouraging children to listen to their bodies and eat until they are satisfied can also help promote healthy eating habits.

In addition to nutrition, regular physical activity is essential for children's health and well-being. It is recommended that children engage in at least 60 minutes of moderate to vigorous physical activity each day.

Parents and caregivers can help children stay active by providing opportunities for outdoor play, enrolling them in sports or recreational activities, and setting a positive example by being physically active themselves. It is important to make physical activity fun and enjoyable for children, as this will help them develop a lifelong love of exercise. Encouraging children to try new activities and explore different types of physical activity can help them find activities that they enjoy and that fit their interests and abilities.

In addition to regular physical activity, it is important for children to engage in age-appropriate strength training exercises to help build muscle and bone strength. Strength training exercises should be performed under the supervision of a qualified fitness professional to ensure safety and proper form. It is important to start with light weights or resistance bands and gradually increase the intensity of the exercises as children grow and develop. By providing a well-balanced diet, encouraging regular physical activity, and promoting healthy habits, parents and caregivers can help children develop strong, healthy bodies and establish lifelong habits of health and wellness. By prioritizing nutrition and exercise for children, we can help set them on a path to a lifetime of good health and well-being.

- Sleep habits and routines

Sleep habits and routines play a crucial role in our overall health and well-being. As creatures of habit, our bodies thrive on consistency, especially when it comes to sleep. The National Sleep Foundation recommends that adults aim for 7-9 hours of quality sleep each night for optimal functioning. However, many individuals struggle to achieve this recommended amount, leading to a host of negative consequences such as impaired cognitive function, decreased productivity, and increased risk of chronic health conditions.

One of the key factors that influence our sleep habits and routines is our internal body clock, also known as our circadian rhythm. This internal clock regulates our sleep-wake cycle and is influenced by external factors such as light and temperature. Exposure to natural light during the day helps to regulate our circadian rhythm, signaling to our body when it is time to be awake and alert. On the other hand, exposure to artificial light, particularly blue light emitted by screens, can disrupt our internal clock and make it difficult to fall asleep at night.

In addition to light exposure, our daily routines and habits also play a significant role in determining the quality of our sleep. Consistency is key when it comes to sleep routines, as going to bed and waking up at the same time each day helps to regulate our internal clock and improve the quality of our sleep.

Creating a bedtime routine that includes relaxing activities such as reading or listening to calming music can also signal to our body that it is time to wind down and prepare for sleep.

It is also important to create a sleep-conducive environment in order to optimize the quality of our sleep. This includes keeping the bedroom cool, dark, and quiet, as well as investing in a comfortable mattress and pillows. Limiting the use of electronic devices in the bedroom can also help to create a more restful sleep environment, as the blue light emitted by screens can interfere with the production of the hormone melatonin, which is essential for regulating our sleep-wake cycle.

In addition to creating a sleep-friendly environment, it is important to establish healthy sleep habits throughout the day in order to improve the quality of our sleep. Regular exercise can help to promote better sleep by reducing stress and anxiety, as well as regulating our body temperature and hormone levels. However, it is important to avoid vigorous exercise close to bedtime, as this can actually interfere with our ability to fall asleep.

Another important factor that can influence our sleep quality is our diet and hydration. Consuming caffeine, alcohol, and heavy meals close to bedtime can disrupt our sleep by interfering with our body's ability to relax and unwind. It is important to be mindful of what we eat and drink in the hours leading up to bedtime in order to promote restful sleep. By establishing consistent bedtime routines, creating a sleep-conducive environment, and practicing healthy habits throughout the day, we can optimize our sleep and improve our overall well-being. It is important to prioritize sleep as a key component of a healthy lifestyle and make the necessary adjustments to ensure that we are getting the quality and quantity of sleep we need to thrive.

- Limiting screen time

Limiting screen time has become a topic of increasing concern in recent years, as the prevalence of technology in our daily lives continues to grow. With the rise of smartphones, tablets, computers, and televisions, many individuals find themselves spending a significant amount of time glued to screens each day.

While technology has brought many benefits, such as increased connectivity and access to information, excessive screen time can have detrimental effects on our physical and mental well-being.

One of the primary reasons for limiting screen time is the impact it can have on our physical health. Prolonged periods of screen use can lead to eye strain, headaches, and neck and back pain. Additionally, excessive screen time has been linked to a sedentary lifestyle, which can contribute to weight gain and an increased risk of obesity. It is important to take regular breaks from screens and engage in physical activity to maintain overall health and well-being.

In addition to physical health concerns, excessive screen time can also have negative effects on our mental well-being. Research has shown that spending too much time on screens can lead to decreased concentration, memory problems, and difficulty sleeping. The constant barrage of information and stimuli from screens can also increase feelings of stress and anxiety. By limiting screen time, individuals can protect their mental health and improve their overall quality of life.

Another important reason to limit screen time is the impact it can have on relationships. Excessive screen use can lead to decreased face-to-face social interactions and a reliance on digital communication. This can hinder the development of meaningful relationships and lead to feelings of isolation and loneliness. By prioritizing time spent with loved ones and engaging in activities that foster connection and communication, individuals can strengthen their relationships and create a more fulfilling and balanced life.

It is worth noting that not all screen time is created equal. While excessive use of screens for entertainment, such as watching television or playing video games, can have negative effects, there are also many benefits to using screens for educational and productive purposes. For example, screens can be valuable tools for learning, communication, and productivity. It is important to strike a balance between using screens for beneficial purposes and limiting screen time to avoid the potential negative consequences.

To effectively limit screen time, individuals can take proactive steps to set boundaries and establish healthy habits. This may include setting specific times of day for screen use, such as creating a "screen-free" hour before bedtime, or designating certain days as "tech-free" days. It can also be helpful to engage in alternative activities that promote well-being, such as exercise, reading, or spending time outdoors. By consciously making choices to reduce screen time and prioritize other activities, individuals can achieve a healthier balance in their lives. By being mindful of the potential negative effects of excessive screen use and taking proactive steps to set boundaries and establish healthy habits, individuals can protect their physical and mental health, strengthen relationships, and create a more balanced and fulfilling life. By finding a balance between using screens for productive purposes and limiting screen time for leisure and entertainment, individuals can enjoy the benefits of technology while also prioritizing their well-being.

Chapter 6: Encouraging Independence

- Fostering self-esteem

Self-esteem is a crucial aspect of an individual's mental and emotional well-being. It refers to the overall opinion we have of ourselves and our abilities. Fostering self-esteem is essential in order to lead a fulfilling and successful life. It allows us to have confidence in ourselves, set and achieve goals, and maintain healthy relationships with others. In this article, we will explore the importance of self-esteem, factors that contribute to its development, and strategies for fostering and improving it.

One of the key reasons why fostering self-esteem is important is because it affects every aspect of our lives. Individuals with high self-esteem are more likely to take risks, try new things, and persevere in the face of challenges. They are also better able to handle criticism, accept failure, and bounce back from setbacks. On the other hand, individuals with low self-esteem are more likely to doubt their abilities, avoid challenges, and struggle with feelings of inadequacy. This can lead to a negative cycle of self-doubt and insecurity that hinders personal growth and success.

There are several factors that contribute to the development of self-esteem. One of the most important factors is our upbringing and early experiences. Children who receive love, support, and encouragement from their parents and caregivers are more likely to develop healthy self-esteem. On the other hand, children who experience neglect, abuse, or criticism may develop low self-esteem. Other factors that can influence self-esteem include social relationships, cultural norms, media influences, and personal achievements.

In order to foster and improve self-esteem, it is important to engage in self-reflection and self-awareness. This involves taking the time to understand and appreciate our strengths, weaknesses, values, and beliefs. By identifying our core values and beliefs, we can cultivate a sense of purpose and direction in our lives. This can help us to make decisions that are aligned with our values and goals, leading to a greater sense of fulfillment and satisfaction.

Another strategy for fostering self-esteem is to practice self-compassion and self-care. This involves treating ourselves with kindness, understanding, and forgiveness. It means acknowledging our flaws and imperfections without judgment or criticism. By practicing self-compassion, we can develop a more positive and loving relationship with ourselves. This can help us to overcome feelings of shame, guilt, and self-criticism, and to embrace our true selves with all of our strengths and weaknesses.

Building healthy relationships with others is also important for fostering self-esteem. Surrounding ourselves with supportive and nurturing people can help us to feel valued, respected, and appreciated. These relationships can provide us with emotional support, encouragement, and validation. They can also serve as a mirror, reflecting back to us our worth and potential. By cultivating positive relationships with others, we can strengthen our self-esteem and sense of belonging.

Engaging in activities that bring us joy, fulfillment, and a sense of accomplishment can also help to foster self-esteem. This can include pursuing hobbies, interests, and passions that align with our values and goals. By setting and achieving personal goals, we can build a sense of mastery and confidence in our abilities. This can help us to develop a positive self-image and a sense of self-worth. It is important to celebrate our successes, big and small, and to acknowledge our progress and growth along the way. It is important to recognize the value and worth inherent in each of us, regardless of our flaws or imperfections. By practicing self-compassion, building positive relationships, and engaging in activities that bring us joy and fulfillment, we can cultivate a strong sense of self-esteem. This can empower us to lead fulfilling and successful lives, to pursue our passions and dreams, and to thrive in the face of challenges and adversity. Remember, you are worthy, capable, and deserving of love and respect, both from yourself and from others.

- Teaching responsibility

Teaching responsibility is a crucial aspect of education that goes beyond academic knowledge. It is about instilling in students the importance of accountability, reliability, and ethical behavior in all aspects of their lives. By teaching responsibility, educators aim to equip students with the skills needed to navigate the challenges of adulthood and become productive members of society.

One key aspect of teaching responsibility is promoting self-discipline and self-control. By teaching students to take responsibility for their actions and decisions, educators help them develop the ability to regulate their behavior and make wise choices. This involves teaching students the importance of setting goals, prioritizing tasks, and managing their time effectively. By instilling these skills, educators empower students to take ownership of their actions and outcomes, leading to greater success in both academic and personal endeavors.

Another important aspect of teaching responsibility is promoting ethical behavior and integrity. Educators play a crucial role in shaping students' moral compass and guiding them to make ethical decisions in all aspects of their lives. By teaching the importance of honesty, fairness, and respect for others, educators help students develop a strong sense of integrity and ethical consciousness. This not only enhances students' personal character but also ensures that they are able to contribute positively to their communities and workplaces.

In addition to promoting self-discipline and ethical behavior, teaching responsibility also involves fostering a sense of accountability and reliability in students. Educators teach students to take ownership of their commitments and fulfill their responsibilities in a timely and dependable manner. By emphasizing the importance of keeping promises, meeting deadlines, and honoring commitments, educators help students build a reputation as trustworthy and reliable individuals. This not only enhances students' chances for success in their academic and professional pursuits but also strengthens their relationships with others.

Teaching responsibility also involves fostering a sense of social responsibility in students. Educators help students recognize the impact of their actions on the world around them and encourage them to contribute positively to their communities. By teaching students the importance of empathy, compassion, and altruism, educators empower them to become active participants in creating a more just and equitable society. This can involve engaging in community service projects, advocating for social justice issues, or simply treating others with kindness and respect. By instilling a sense of social responsibility in students, educators help them become responsible citizens who are committed to making a positive difference in the world. It is about instilling in students the values of accountability, reliability, and ethical behavior that are essential for success in all aspects of their lives. By promoting self-discipline, ethical behavior, accountability, and social responsibility, educators play a crucial role in shaping students' character and preparing them to navigate the challenges of adulthood with integrity and resilience. Through their guidance and mentorship, educators help students develop the skills and mindset needed to become responsible individuals who make meaningful contributions to their communities and the world at large.

- Allowing room for growth and mistakes

Allowing room for growth and mistakes is essential in any learning environment, whether it be in the classroom, workplace, or personal life. By creating a safe space for individuals to make mistakes and learn from them, we are fostering a culture of growth and continuous improvement. This concept is rooted in the idea that we are all human and that making mistakes is an inevitable part of the learning process. Instead of shaming individuals for their mistakes, we should embrace them as opportunities for learning and development.

In the academic setting, allowing room for growth and mistakes is crucial for students to reach their full potential. When students feel pressured to be perfect and fear making mistakes, they are less likely to take risks and explore new ideas. By creating an environment where mistakes are seen as valuable learning opportunities, students are more likely to take ownership of their learning and push themselves to new heights. Teachers play a key role in this process by providing constructive feedback and guidance to help students learn from their mistakes and grow as learners.

In the workplace, allowing room for growth and mistakes can lead to increased productivity, innovation, and employee morale. When employees feel empowered to take risks and try new things without the fear of punishment or retribution, they are more likely to think creatively and come up with new solutions to problems. It is important for leaders to create a culture that encourages experimentation and learning from mistakes, rather than punishing or shaming employees for errors. By fostering a culture of growth and development, organizations can create a more dynamic and resilient workforce.

On a personal level, allowing room for growth and mistakes is essential for individual growth and self-improvement. It is natural to make mistakes and encounter setbacks in life, but it is how we respond to these challenges that determines our growth and development. By embracing our mistakes and learning from them, we can become more resilient, adaptable, and self-aware individuals. It is important to practice self-compassion and forgiveness when we make mistakes, and to see them as opportunities for growth rather than failures. By creating an environment where individuals feel safe to make mistakes and learn from them, we can encourage creativity, innovation, and personal growth. Whether in the classroom, workplace, or personal life, it is important to embrace mistakes as opportunities for learning and to support others in their journey of growth and development. As we strive for excellence and continuous improvement, let us remember that mistakes are an inevitable and valuable part of the learning process.

Chapter 7: Handling Challenging Behaviors

- Dealing with tantrums

Tantrums are a common behavior exhibited by many children, typically between the ages of 1 and 4 years old. They are characterized by an outburst of anger or frustration, often accompanied by crying, screaming, kicking, or throwing objects. Tantrums can be challenging for parents to deal with, as they can be disruptive and difficult to manage. However, it is important to understand that tantrums are a normal part of child development and are not indicative of a child's character or behavior.

One of the key strategies for dealing with tantrums is to remain calm and composed when a child is having a tantrum. It can be tempting to respond with anger or frustration, but this will only escalate the situation and make it harder to resolve. Instead, take a deep breath and try to stay calm and patient. Remember that tantrums are a normal part of child development and that your child is not deliberately trying to upset you.

Another important strategy for dealing with tantrums is to identify the triggers that may be causing them. Tantrums can be triggered by a variety of factors, such as hunger, tiredness, overstimulation, or frustration. By identifying the triggers that set off your child's tantrums, you can work to prevent them from occurring in the future. For example, if your child tends to have tantrums when they are hungry, make sure to have healthy snacks available to keep their energy levels up.

It is also essential to set clear boundaries and expectations for your child's behavior. Establishing rules and limits can help prevent tantrums by providing structure and consistency for your child. Make sure to communicate these boundaries to your child in a calm and consistent manner, and reinforce them with positive reinforcement when they follow the rules. By setting clear boundaries and expectations, you can help your child understand what is expected of them and reduce the likelihood of tantrums occurring.

When dealing with a tantrum, it is important to remember that your child is likely feeling overwhelmed and frustrated. Instead of punishing or scolding them for their behavior, try to empathize with them and help them work through their emotions. Encourage them to use words to express their feelings and provide support and reassurance as they calm down. By showing empathy and understanding, you can help your child feel safe and secure, which can help reduce the intensity and duration of their tantrum.

It is also essential to remember that consistency is key when dealing with tantrums. By responding to tantrums in a consistent and predictable manner, you can help your child understand the consequences of their behavior and learn how to regulate their emotions. Make sure to follow through on any consequences or rewards that you have established for your child's behavior, and be consistent in your response to tantrums. By setting clear expectations and sticking to them, you can help your child learn to manage their emotions and behavior effectively. By remaining calm and composed, identifying triggers, setting clear boundaries, showing empathy and understanding, and being consistent in your response, you can help your child learn to manage their emotions and behavior effectively. Remember that parenting is a journey, and it is okay to seek support and guidance when needed. By taking a proactive and positive approach to dealing with tantrums, you can help your child develop the skills they need to navigate their emotions and behaviors successfully.

- Conflict resolution strategies

Conflict resolution strategies are essential tools for navigating disagreements and disputes in both personal and professional settings. Conflict is an inevitable part of human interaction, and the ability to effectively resolve conflicts is a valuable skill that can lead to improved relationships, increased productivity, and a more positive work environment. In this essay, we will explore a variety of conflict resolution strategies, including negotiation, mediation, and collaboration, and discuss how these approaches can be applied in different situations to achieve mutually beneficial outcomes.

Negotiation is perhaps the most commonly used conflict resolution strategy, involving a process of bargaining and compromise to reach a mutually acceptable solution. In negotiation, parties with opposing interests come together to discuss their respective needs and preferences and work towards finding a middle ground that satisfies both sides. Effective negotiation requires good communication skills, empathy, and a willingness to listen and understand the other party's perspective. By focusing on interests rather than positions, negotiators can often uncover common ground and identify creative solutions that meet the needs of all parties involved.

Mediation is another valuable conflict resolution strategy that involves the use of a neutral third party to facilitate communication and help parties reach a resolution. Mediators are trained professionals who can impartially listen to both sides, clarify issues, and guide the discussion towards a mutually acceptable agreement. Mediation is particularly useful in situations where there is a significant power imbalance or where emotions are running high. By providing a safe and structured environment for communication, mediators can help parties overcome barriers to resolution and find common ground.

Collaboration is a conflict resolution strategy that focuses on working together to find a solution that benefits all parties involved. Unlike negotiation, which often involves some level of compromise, collaboration seeks to identify win-win solutions that satisfy everyone's interests. Collaborative conflict resolution requires a high degree of trust, transparency, and a willingness to work towards a common goal. By fostering a spirit of cooperation and shared responsibility, collaborators can build stronger relationships and create lasting solutions that address the underlying causes of conflict.

In addition to negotiation, mediation, and collaboration, there are several other conflict resolution strategies that can be effective in different situations. For example, arbitration involves the use of a neutral third party to make a binding decision on the outcome of a dispute, which can be particularly useful when parties are unable to reach an agreement through negotiation or mediation.

Avoidance is another strategy that involves ignoring or avoiding conflict altogether, which can be appropriate in certain situations where the issue is not important or when emotions are running too high to have a productive conversation.

When choosing a conflict resolution strategy, it is important to consider the specific circumstances of the conflict and the needs and preferences of the parties involved. Different strategies may be more appropriate depending on the nature of the conflict, the relationship between the parties, and the desired outcome. It is also important to remember that conflict resolution is not always about finding a quick fix or a one-size-fits-all solution. It is about engaging in a process of communication, negotiation, and problem-solving that can lead to a deeper understanding of the underlying issues and ultimately create a stronger foundation for future interactions. By choosing the right strategy and approaching conflict with an open mind and a willingness to listen and collaborate, parties can work towards finding mutually beneficial solutions that promote understanding, respect, and cooperation. Whether through negotiation, mediation, collaboration, or another approach, effective conflict resolution can lead to stronger relationships, increased productivity, and a more positive and harmonious work environment. By honing our conflict resolution skills and embracing a spirit of openness and cooperation, we can navigate conflicts with confidence and create a more peaceful and productive world for ourselves and others.

- Managing sibling rivalry

Sibling rivalry is a common phenomenon that occurs within families when siblings compete for attention, resources, and recognition from their parents. This rivalry can manifest in various forms, such as arguing, fighting, and trying to outdo one another in different aspects of their lives. While sibling rivalry is a normal part of growing up, it can also cause tension and conflict within the family if not managed effectively. In this essay, we will explore the causes of sibling rivalry, its impact on family dynamics, and strategies for parents to effectively manage and reduce sibling rivalry in their children.

One of the main causes of sibling rivalry is the natural desire for attention and approval from parents. Children seek validation and recognition from their parents, and when they feel that their siblings are receiving more attention or praise, they may become jealous or resentful. This can lead to feelings of inadequacy and a desire to compete with their siblings for the limited resources of their parents' time and attention. Additionally, sibling rivalry can be fueled by differences in personality, interests, and abilities between siblings, as they may feel the need to prove themselves or establish their own identity in relation to their siblings.

Sibling rivalry can have a significant impact on family dynamics, creating tension and conflict among siblings and between parents and children. Siblings may argue, fight, and engage in power struggles in an attempt to establish dominance and assert their individuality within the family. This can lead to a breakdown in communication, a lack of cooperation, and a negative atmosphere within the household. Parents may also feel overwhelmed and stressed by the constant bickering and competition between their children, leading to feelings of frustration and helplessness.

In order to effectively manage and reduce sibling rivalry, parents can employ a variety of strategies to promote positive sibling relationships and create a harmonious family environment. One key strategy is to encourage open communication and collaboration among siblings, fostering a sense of teamwork and mutual support. Parents can also help their children develop conflict resolution skills and empathy, teaching them how to express their feelings and resolve disagreements in a constructive and respectful manner. By modeling and reinforcing positive behavior, parents can help their children learn how to work through conflicts and build strong, supportive relationships with their siblings.

Another important strategy for managing sibling rivalry is to establish clear and consistent rules and boundaries within the family. By setting expectations for behavior and consequences for breaking rules, parents can create a sense of fairness and equality among siblings, reducing the likelihood of disputes and power struggles. Parents can also promote individuality and independence by recognizing and celebrating the unique strengths and talents of each child, fostering a sense of self-worth and confidence in their abilities.

Furthermore, parents can foster positive sibling relationships by creating opportunities for their children to bond and connect with one another. Family activities, such as game nights, outings, and vacations, can help siblings develop shared interests and experiences, strengthening their bond and promoting cooperation and mutual respect. By encouraging positive interactions and fostering a sense of belonging within the family, parents can help reduce feelings of jealousy and competition among siblings, fostering a sense of unity and camaraderie within the household. By understanding the causes of sibling rivalry and implementing effective strategies for managing and reducing conflicts, parents can promote positive sibling relationships and create a harmonious and supportive family environment. By fostering communication, cooperation, and mutual respect among siblings, parents can help their children build strong, lasting relationships that will withstand the challenges and conflicts of sibling rivalry. Through patience, consistency, and love, parents can create a nurturing and supportive family environment in which siblings can thrive and grow together.

Chapter 8: Effective Communication

- Active listening skills

Active listening skills are essential in both professional and personal settings. By actively listening to others, we can demonstrate empathy, build trust, and foster strong relationships. Active listening involves not only hearing what someone is saying but also understanding their emotions, thoughts, and perspectives. This requires full engagement and focus on the speaker, without distractions or interruptions. Active listening is a skill that can be developed through practice and attention to key techniques.

One important aspect of active listening is giving the speaker your full attention. This means making eye contact, nodding, and responding appropriately to show that you are actively engaged in the conversation. It is important to avoid distractions such as looking at your phone or checking your watch while someone is speaking. By giving the speaker your full attention, you are signaling that you value what they have to say and are interested in understanding their point of view.

Another key element of active listening is paraphrasing or summarizing what the speaker has said. This shows that you have been paying attention and have understood the main points of their message. By paraphrasing, you can also clarify any misunderstandings or misinterpretations that may have arisen during the conversation. This can help to ensure that both parties are on the same page and can move the conversation forward in a productive manner.

Reflecting back the speaker's emotions and feelings is also an important aspect of active listening. This involves acknowledging and validating the speaker's emotions, even if you may not agree with their perspective. By showing empathy and understanding, you can create a supportive and safe environment for the speaker to express themselves openly and honestly. This can help to deepen the connection between you and the speaker and build trust in the relationship.

Active listening also involves asking open-ended questions to encourage the speaker to share more about their thoughts and feelings. Open-ended questions prompt the speaker to elaborate on their ideas and provide more insight into their perspective. By asking thoughtful and probing questions, you can show that you are genuinely interested in understanding the speaker's point of view and are willing to engage in a meaningful dialogue. This can help to build rapport and trust in the conversation.

In addition to verbal cues, nonverbal cues are also important in active listening. Nonverbal cues such as body language, facial expressions, and gestures can convey your interest and engagement in the conversation. By leaning in, making eye contact, and nodding, you can show that you are attentive and receptive to what the speaker is saying. Nonverbal cues can also help to create a positive and supportive atmosphere for the speaker to feel comfortable sharing their thoughts and feelings. By giving the speaker your full attention, paraphrasing their message, reflecting back their emotions, asking open-ended questions, and using nonverbal cues, you can demonstrate empathy, build trust, and create a strong connection with others. Practice these active listening techniques regularly to improve your communication skills and deepen your relationships with colleagues, friends, and family members.

- Expressing emotions calmly

Expressing emotions calmly is an essential skill that can greatly benefit individuals in both their personal and professional lives. When emotions run high, it can be easy to react impulsively, saying or doing things that we later regret. However, by learning to express emotions in a calm and collected manner, we can communicate effectively, manage conflicts constructively, and build stronger relationships with others.

One key aspect of expressing emotions calmly is self-awareness. Before reacting to a situation, take a moment to pause and check in with yourself. Identify the emotions you are feeling and consider the root cause of these emotions.

By understanding your own emotional triggers, you can better control your reactions and choose a more measured response. This self-awareness also allows you to express your emotions in a way that is genuine and authentic, rather than letting them escalate into unproductive outbursts.

In addition to self-awareness, it is important to practice emotional regulation techniques to help you stay calm in challenging situations. Deep breathing exercises, mindfulness meditation, and progressive muscle relaxation are all effective ways to manage stress and anxiety, allowing you to approach difficult conversations with a clear and focused mind. By incorporating these techniques into your daily routine, you can cultivate a sense of emotional resilience that will serve you well in any situation.

When it comes to expressing emotions calmly, communication is key. Clearly and assertively communicate your feelings using "I" statements, which focus on your own emotions rather than blaming others. For example, instead of saying "You always make me so angry," try saying "I feel frustrated when this happens. " By taking ownership of your emotions and expressing them in a non-confrontational way, you can create a space for open and honest dialogue with others.

Active listening is another important aspect of expressing emotions calmly. When someone else is expressing their emotions, take the time to listen attentively, without interrupting or formulating a response in your mind. Reflect back what the other person is saying to show that you understand and empathize with their perspective. By practicing active listening, you can foster a sense of mutual respect and understanding in your interactions with others, leading to more productive and harmonious relationships.

Conflict resolution is often a challenging situation where expressing emotions calmly can make a significant difference. When faced with a conflict, take the time to understand the other person's perspective, even if you disagree with it. Avoid reacting impulsively or defensively, and instead, strive to find common ground and work towards a mutually beneficial solution. By approaching conflicts with a calm and rational mindset, you can de-escalate tension and build trust and collaboration with others. By practicing self-awareness, emotional regulation, effective communication, active listening, and conflict resolution techniques, you can cultivate an emotional intelligence that will serve you well in any situation. Remember that it is okay to feel and express your emotions, but by doing so in a calm and collected manner, you can navigate difficult situations with grace and integrity.

- Resolving conflicts peacefully

Conflict resolution is an essential skill in both personal and professional settings. It involves addressing and resolving disagreements or disputes in a peaceful and constructive manner. By approaching conflicts with a positive and open-minded attitude, individuals can find mutually acceptable solutions that benefit all parties involved. In this discussion, we will explore the importance of resolving conflicts peacefully, the key principles of conflict resolution, and practical strategies for effectively managing conflicts.

Peaceful conflict resolution is crucial for maintaining healthy relationships, whether it be with family members, friends, colleagues, or even strangers. When conflicts arise, they can create tension, misunderstandings, and breakdown in communication if not properly addressed. By resolving conflicts peacefully, individuals can prevent further escalation, promote understanding, and strengthen relationships. Conflict resolution allows individuals to work through disagreements in a respectful and empathetic manner, leading to improved communication, trust, and cooperation among all parties involved.

There are several key principles that underpin successful conflict resolution. Firstly, it is important to approach conflicts with an open mind and willingness to listen to the perspectives of others. By actively listening and seeking to understand the underlying interests and needs of all parties, individuals can gain greater insight into the root causes of the conflict and work towards finding mutually beneficial solutions. Secondly, maintaining respect and civility throughout the conflict resolution process is essential. Treating others with dignity and respect, even in the heat of a disagreement, helps to create a positive and constructive atmosphere for resolving conflicts.

Effective communication is another crucial aspect of peaceful conflict resolution. Clear and honest communication plays a vital role in addressing misunderstandings, clarifying expectations, and expressing needs and concerns. By effectively communicating their thoughts and feelings, individuals can prevent misunderstandings, build trust, and foster empathy towards each other's perspectives. In addition, active listening is a key component of effective communication in conflict resolution. By listening attentively to the concerns and viewpoints of others, individuals demonstrate empathy and understanding, which can help to de-escalate conflicts and facilitate the search for common ground.

Furthermore, creativity and flexibility are essential skills in resolving conflicts peacefully. By thinking creatively and exploring various options and solutions, individuals can find innovative ways to address the underlying issues and meet the needs of all parties involved. Flexibility is also important in conflict resolution, as it allows individuals to adapt and adjust their approach to the changing dynamics of a conflict. By being open to new ideas and willing to compromise, individuals can find mutually acceptable solutions that satisfy the interests of all parties without sacrificing their own needs and values.

In practice, there are several strategies that individuals can employ to effectively resolve conflicts peacefully. Firstly, it is important to address conflicts in a timely manner before they escalate and cause irreparable damage to relationships. By addressing conflicts early on, individuals can prevent misunderstandings and grievances from festering and becoming more difficult to resolve. Secondly, individuals should approach conflicts with a collaborative mindset, seeking to find solutions that benefit all parties involved rather than focusing on winning or being right. By working together to find common ground and build consensus, individuals can create win-win outcomes that satisfy the needs and interests of all parties.

Moreover, individuals should engage in active and empathetic listening during conflict resolution to demonstrate understanding and validation towards the concerns and perspectives of others. By actively listening and acknowledging the emotions and needs of all parties involved, individuals can foster trust, empathy, and cooperation, leading to a more constructive and positive resolution of conflicts. In addition, individuals should strive to maintain a calm and respectful demeanor throughout the conflict resolution process, avoiding personal attacks, blaming, or defensiveness. By staying composed and focused on the issues at hand, individuals can create a safe and supportive environment for open and honest communication, paving the way for a peaceful resolution of conflicts. By approaching conflicts with an open mind, respectful attitude, and effective communication skills, individuals can navigate disagreements and disputes in a constructive and positive manner. By following the key principles of conflict resolution and employing practical strategies, individuals can effectively manage conflicts and find mutually beneficial solutions that satisfy the needs and interests of all parties. Peaceful conflict resolution is not only important for maintaining harmonious relationships but also for fostering a culture of respect, empathy, and collaboration in all aspects of life.

Chapter 9: Nurturing Emotional Intelligence

- Teaching empathy and compassion

Empathy and compassion are essential qualities that should be imparted to students through effective teaching methods. Empathy is the ability to understand and share the feelings of another person, while compassion is the desire to alleviate the suffering of others. These two qualities go hand in hand and are crucial for creating a more harmonious and empathetic society.

Teaching empathy and compassion in the classroom can have a positive impact on students' social and emotional development. It helps them to understand and appreciate different perspectives, leading to better communication and interpersonal relationships. When students are able to put themselves in someone else's shoes, they are more likely to show kindness, understanding, and respect towards others.

One of the most effective ways to teach empathy and compassion is through modeling. Teachers who demonstrate empathy and compassion towards their students create a safe and nurturing environment where students feel valued and understood. By showing empathy and compassion in their interactions with students, teachers set an example for their students to follow and encourage them to develop these qualities in themselves.

In addition to modeling, educators can also teach empathy and compassion through direct instruction. This can involve discussing real-life situations where empathy and compassion were demonstrated, engaging students in role-playing exercises, and encouraging students to reflect on their own experiences and feelings. By providing students with opportunities to practice empathy and compassion, teachers can help them develop these important social and emotional skills.

Another important aspect of teaching empathy and compassion is fostering a sense of community in the classroom. When students feel connected to their peers and teachers, they are more likely to show empathy and compassion towards others. Teachers can create a sense of community by promoting teamwork, encouraging collaboration, and providing opportunities for students to work together towards common goals.

It is also important for educators to emphasize the importance of empathy and compassion in the curriculum. By integrating lessons on empathy and compassion into various subjects, teachers can help students see the relevance of these qualities in all aspects of their lives. For example, teachers can incorporate literature that highlights the importance of empathy and compassion, or encourage students to research and discuss current events where empathy and compassion are needed.

Furthermore, teachers can also help students develop empathy and compassion by encouraging them to engage in community service and volunteer work. By participating in activities that involve helping others, students can gain a deeper understanding of the challenges faced by different individuals and develop a greater sense of empathy and compassion. Teachers can support students in finding volunteer opportunities and provide guidance on how to make a positive impact in their communities. By modeling these qualities, providing direct instruction, fostering a sense of community, integrating lessons into the curriculum, and encouraging students to engage in community service, educators can help students develop the social and emotional skills needed to show empathy and compassion towards others. Through these efforts, teachers can play a crucial role in shaping the next generation of empathetic and compassionate individuals.

- Helping children manage emotions

Emotions are a key aspect of human experience, and they play a crucial role in our daily lives. For children, learning how to manage their emotions is an essential skill that can have a significant impact on their overall well-being and success. As children grow and develop, they are constantly faced with new challenges and experiences that can evoke a wide range of emotions. From joy and excitement to frustration and sadness, children must learn how to navigate these emotions in a healthy and constructive way.

One of the most important aspects of helping children manage their emotions is teaching them to recognize and identify what they are feeling. This may seem simple, but for young children who are still developing their emotional vocabulary, it can be a challenging task. Parents and caregivers can help by using words to describe emotions and asking children to identify how they are feeling in different situations. By helping children label their emotions, adults can empower them to better understand and express their feelings.

Once children are able to recognize and label their emotions, the next step is teaching them how to regulate and manage these feelings. Emotion regulation is a complex skill that involves being able to control and modulate one's emotions in response to different situations. For children, this may involve learning strategies such as deep breathing, taking a break, or talking to a trusted adult when they are feeling overwhelmed. By providing children with tools and techniques to regulate their emotions, adults can help them develop the resilience and coping skills needed to navigate life's ups and downs.

In addition to teaching children how to recognize and regulate their emotions, it is also important to help them understand that all feelings are valid and that it is okay to express them. Children should be encouraged to talk about their emotions openly and honestly, without fear of judgment or criticism. By creating a safe and supportive environment for children to express themselves, adults can help them develop a healthy relationship with their emotions and learn how to communicate their feelings effectively.

When children are struggling to manage their emotions, it is important for adults to provide guidance and support. This may involve helping children identify the root cause of their feelings, brainstorming potential solutions, or simply offering a listening ear. By showing empathy and understanding, adults can help children feel heard and validated, which can in turn help them process and move through their emotions in a constructive way.

It is also important for adults to model healthy emotional regulation and expression for children. Children learn by example, so it is essential for adults to demonstrate how to cope with and manage their own emotions in a positive and respectful manner. By showing children that it is okay to feel emotions and that there are healthy ways to respond to them, adults can empower children to develop their own emotional intelligence and resilience. By teaching children to recognize, regulate, and express their emotions in a healthy and constructive way, adults can empower children to navigate life's challenges with resilience and confidence. By providing guidance, support, and positive role modeling, adults can help children develop the skills and tools they need to become emotionally intelligent individuals who are able to thrive in an ever-changing world.

- Coping with stress and anxiety

In today's fast-paced and demanding world, it is no surprise that many individuals are struggling with stress and anxiety. Whether it is due to work pressures, personal relationships, or financial concerns, the constant barrage of stressors can take a toll on our mental and physical well-being. Coping with stress and anxiety is an essential skill that everyone should have in their arsenal, as these conditions can have a significant impact on our overall quality of life.

Stress is a natural response to challenging situations, and in small doses, it can actually be beneficial as it can motivate us to take action and overcome obstacles. However, when stress becomes chronic or overwhelming, it can lead to a variety of negative consequences, including anxiety, depression, and physical health problems. Learning how to effectively cope with stress is crucial in order to prevent these adverse outcomes and maintain a sense of balance and well-being in our lives.

One of the first steps in coping with stress and anxiety is to identify the sources of our stress and understand how they are impacting us. This may require some self-reflection and introspection, as it can sometimes be difficult to pinpoint exactly what is causing our stress. Keeping a journal or engaging in therapy can be helpful in this process, as it can allow us to explore our thoughts and feelings in a safe and supportive environment. Once we have a better understanding of the sources of our stress, we can begin to develop strategies for managing and reducing it.

There are a variety of techniques that can be effective in coping with stress and anxiety, and it is important to find the ones that work best for you. Some people may find relief through exercise, meditation, or relaxation techniques such as deep breathing or progressive muscle relaxation. Others may benefit from engaging in creative activities, spending time in nature, or connecting with loved ones. It is important to experiment with different strategies and find what works best for you, as everyone is unique and what works for one person may not work for another.

In addition to finding coping strategies that work for you, it is also important to take care of your physical health in order to better cope with stress and anxiety. This includes getting regular exercise, eating a healthy diet, getting enough sleep, and avoiding substances such as alcohol and caffeine that can exacerbate stress and anxiety. Taking care of your physical health can help to improve your overall well-being and resilience in the face of stressors.

It is also important to reach out for support when coping with stress and anxiety. This may mean talking to a trusted friend or family member about what you are going through, seeking support from a therapist or counselor, or connecting with a support group. It is important to remember that you are not alone in your struggles, and there are many resources available to help you navigate difficult times. Seeking support can help you to feel heard, understood, and validated, which can be incredibly comforting when dealing with stress and anxiety. By identifying the sources of our stress, developing effective coping strategies, taking care of our physical health, and reaching out for support when needed, we can better navigate the challenges that life throws our way. Remember that it is okay to ask for help and that you are not alone in your struggles. With the right tools and support, you can learn to manage your stress and anxiety in a healthy and productive way.

Chapter 10: Encouraging Creativity and Exploration

- Providing opportunities for creativity

Providing opportunities for creativity is essential in fostering innovation, problem-solving skills, and personal growth. Creativity is the ability to think outside the box, come up with new ideas, and connect seemingly unrelated concepts. It is a skill that is highly valued in today's fast-paced and competitive world. By providing opportunities for creativity, individuals can develop their creative thinking skills and learn how to approach challenges in new and inventive ways.

One way to provide opportunities for creativity is through education. Schools and educational institutions can incorporate creative thinking exercises, projects, and assignments into their curriculum to encourage students to think creatively. By exposing students to different ways of approaching problems and tasks, educators can help them develop their creative thinking skills and foster a sense of curiosity and exploration. Additionally, teachers can create a classroom environment that values and celebrates creativity, where students feel empowered to express their ideas and think outside the box.

Another way to provide opportunities for creativity is through the workplace. Employers can support and encourage their employees to think creatively by creating a work culture that values innovation and experimentation. This can be done by offering opportunities for training and development in creative thinking skills, providing resources and tools to support creativity, and recognizing and rewarding creative ideas and solutions. By fostering a culture of creativity in the workplace, employers can tap into the full potential of their employees and drive innovation and growth within the organization.

In addition to education and the workplace, individuals can also create opportunities for creativity in their personal lives. This can be done by engaging in creative hobbies and activities such as painting, writing, cooking, or gardening. These activities can help individuals tap into their creative potential, relax and unwind, and explore new ideas and concepts. By incorporating creativity into their daily lives, individuals can enhance their problem-solving skills, boost their self-confidence, and foster a sense of fulfillment and satisfaction. Whether in education, the workplace, or personal life, creativity plays a vital role in helping individuals think outside the box, come up with new ideas, and approach challenges in new and inventive ways. By creating a supportive environment that values and celebrates creativity, individuals can unleash their creative potential and thrive in today's fast-paced and competitive world.

- Supporting interests and hobbies

Supporting interests and hobbies is an essential aspect of personal development and well-being. Engaging in activities that bring us joy, fulfillment, and a sense of accomplishment can greatly enhance our overall quality of life. Whether it's playing a musical instrument, practicing a sport, painting, gardening, or any other hobby, dedicating time and energy to our interests can have numerous benefits for both our mental and physical health.

One of the key advantages of pursuing interests and hobbies is the opportunity they provide for creativity and self-expression. When we engage in activities that we are passionate about, we are able to tap into our unique skills and talents, and express ourselves in a way that is deeply satisfying. This creative outlet can be a powerful source of stress relief and can help us cultivate a sense of purpose and identity outside of our daily responsibilities.

Furthermore, engaging in hobbies and interests can also contribute to our cognitive development and lifelong learning. Whether we are learning a new language, researching a historical period, or refining our cooking skills, hobbies provide an avenue for intellectual stimulation and growth. By challenging ourselves to acquire new knowledge and skills in a non-academic setting, we can expand our horizons, build self-confidence, and develop problem-solving abilities that can be applied to other areas of our lives.

In addition to the personal benefits of pursuing interests and hobbies, these activities can also have a positive impact on our social connections and relationships. Many hobbies are inherently social, providing opportunities to connect with likeminded individuals, build friendships, and strengthen existing bonds with family and friends. Engaging in shared interests can create a sense of community and belonging, and foster a supportive network of individuals who can provide encouragement, feedback, and camaraderie.

However, despite the many benefits of pursuing interests and hobbies, it can sometimes be challenging to prioritize and maintain these activities in the midst of our busy lives. Work, family obligations, and other responsibilities can often leave us feeling overwhelmed and exhausted, making it difficult to carve out time for the things that bring us joy. In these situations, it is important to recognize the value of self-care and make a conscious effort to prioritize our own well-being by creating space for our hobbies and interests.

One strategy for supporting interests and hobbies is to establish a routine or schedule that includes dedicated time for these activities. By setting aside specific blocks of time each week for our hobbies, we can ensure that they become a regular part of our lives and are not relegated to the realm of "someday" or "when I have free time." Additionally, involving family members or friends in our hobbies can help to create accountability and motivation, as well as strengthen our relationships through shared experiences.

Another important aspect of supporting interests and hobbies is to seek out resources and opportunities for growth and development within our chosen pursuits. This may involve taking classes or workshops, joining a club or organization, or seeking out mentorship from individuals who are more experienced in our hobby. By investing in our own learning and skill development, we can deepen our engagement with our hobbies and unlock new levels of enjoyment and fulfillment.

Ultimately, supporting interests and hobbies is a valuable investment in our overall well-being and happiness. By dedicating time and energy to the activities that bring us joy and fulfillment, we can enhance our creativity, cognitive abilities, social connections, and sense of purpose. As we navigate the demands of daily life, it is essential to prioritize self-care and make space for the things that nourish our spirits and contribute to our personal growth and development. By cultivating a healthy balance between work, responsibilities, and leisure activities, we can create a fulfilling and meaningful life that is rich in experiences, connections, and personal satisfaction.

- Encouraging curiosity and learning

Encouraging curiosity and learning is essential in fostering intellectual growth and personal development. Curiosity is a natural human trait that drives us to seek out new knowledge and experiences, enabling us to expand our understanding of the world around us. By nurturing and encouraging curiosity in individuals, we can inspire a lifelong love of learning and a thirst for knowledge that can propel them to new heights of achievement. In this essay, we will explore the importance of fostering curiosity and learning, as well as some practical strategies for cultivating these skills in ourselves and others.

One of the key benefits of encouraging curiosity and learning is that it helps to stimulate cognitive development and innovation. When we are curious about a topic, we are more likely to engage with it fully and to seek out new information and perspectives. This process of exploration can lead to new insights and discoveries, helping us to expand our knowledge and deepen our understanding of the world. Moreover, curiosity can also drive innovation by prompting us to ask questions and challenge conventional wisdom, leading to new ideas and solutions to complex problems.

In addition to fostering cognitive development and innovation, encouraging curiosity and learning can also have a positive impact on personal growth and well-being. Curious individuals are more likely to be open-minded and receptive to new ideas, experiences, and perspectives, which can help to broaden their horizons and deepen their understanding of themselves and the world around them. Moreover, engaging in learning activities can help to boost self-confidence and self-esteem, as individuals gain new skills and knowledge that can be applied in various aspects of their lives.

So, how can we go about encouraging curiosity and learning in ourselves and others. One strategy is to create a supportive and stimulating environment that nourishes curiosity and encourages exploration. This can be achieved by providing access to a wide range of resources and opportunities for learning, such as books, workshops, online courses, and hands-on activities. Encouraging individuals to ask questions, think critically, and engage with the material in a deep and meaningful way can also help to foster curiosity and encourage a thirst for knowledge.

Another important strategy for cultivating curiosity and learning is to model these behaviors ourselves. By demonstrating a love of learning and a willingness to explore new ideas and perspectives, we can inspire others to do the same. This can be done through our interactions with others, our choice of reading material, and our approach to problem-solving and decision-making. By showing that we value curiosity and learning, we can help to create a culture that celebrates intellectual growth and personal development. By nurturing these skills in ourselves and others, we can inspire a lifelong love of learning and a thirst for knowledge that can propel us to new heights of achievement. By creating a supportive and stimulating environment, modeling curiosity and learning behaviors, and providing access to resources and opportunities for exploration, we can help to cultivate a culture that celebrates intellectual curiosity and encourages a lifelong quest for knowledge.

Chapter 11: Developing a Strong Parenting Partnership

- Communication with co-parents

Effective communication with co-parents is vital for the well-being and development of children in shared custody arrangements. Co-parenting, which refers to the joint responsibility of caring for children after a separation or divorce, requires ongoing collaboration and coordination between parents. By maintaining open and respectful communication, co-parents can create a supportive and stable environment for their children to thrive.

One key aspect of effective communication with co-parents is establishing clear and consistent channels of communication. This can include in-person meetings, phone calls, emails, texts, or communication through a co-parenting app. By establishing a regular method of communication, co-parents can stay informed about their children's schedules, activities, and well-being. This also helps to prevent misunderstandings and miscommunication, which can create tension and conflict between co-parents.

Another important element of communication with co-parents is maintaining a cooperative and respectful attitude. It is essential for co-parents to set aside their differences and focus on the well-being of their children. By approaching communication with an open mind and a willingness to compromise, co-parents can work together to make decisions that are in the best interest of their children. This may require setting aside personal grievances or emotions in order to prioritize the needs of the children.

Effective communication with co-parents also involves being flexible and adaptable. Life is unpredictable, and circumstances may change that require adjustments to the co-parenting plan. By staying flexible and open to changes, co-parents can work together to find solutions that accommodate everyone's needs. This may involve revisiting the co-parenting agreement periodically to make necessary adjustments based on the children's changing needs and schedules.

Furthermore, active listening is a crucial component of effective communication with co-parents. It is essential for co-parents to listen to each other's perspectives, concerns, and suggestions without interrupting or dismissing them. By actively listening, co-parents can show respect for each other's opinions and work towards finding common ground. This can help to build trust and foster a sense of collaboration between co-parents.

In addition to verbal communication, nonverbal communication also plays a significant role in co-parenting relationships. It is important for co-parents to be aware of their body language, tone of voice, and facial expressions when communicating with each other. Nonverbal cues can convey emotions and attitudes that may not be expressed verbally, so it is important for co-parents to be mindful of how they present themselves during conversations. By being aware of their nonverbal communication, co-parents can avoid sending mixed messages or creating unnecessary tension.

Lastly, setting boundaries and establishing ground rules for communication can help to maintain a healthy co-parenting relationship. It is important for co-parents to respect each other's privacy, space, and time by establishing guidelines for communication. This may include defining when and how communication should take place, as well as establishing boundaries around the topics that are appropriate for discussion. By setting clear boundaries, co-parents can reduce the risk of conflict and maintain a positive and constructive co-parenting relationship. By establishing clear channels of communication, maintaining a cooperative attitude, being flexible and adaptable, actively listening, being mindful of nonverbal cues, and setting boundaries, co-parents can work together to prioritize the well-being and development of their children. By fostering open and respectful communication, co-parents can create a positive and collaborative co-parenting environment that benefits everyone involved.

- Balancing roles and responsibilities

Balancing roles and responsibilities is a crucial aspect of managing one's personal and professional life effectively. In today's fast-paced world, individuals are often juggling multiple roles and responsibilities, from work duties to family commitments and personal interests. Finding a balance between these different aspects of life can be challenging, but it is essential for maintaining overall well-being and achieving long-term success.

One key to balancing roles and responsibilities is effective time management. By prioritizing tasks and allocating time efficiently, individuals can ensure that they are able to fulfill their various obligations without feeling overwhelmed or stressed. This may involve creating a daily or weekly schedule, setting specific goals for each day, and breaking larger tasks into smaller, more manageable steps. By taking a proactive approach to managing their time, individuals can reduce the risk of becoming overwhelmed by their responsibilities and increase their overall productivity.

Another important aspect of balancing roles and responsibilities is setting boundaries. It is essential for individuals to establish clear boundaries between their different roles and responsibilities in order to prevent them from bleeding into one another. For example, it may be helpful to designate specific times for work, family, and personal activities, and to communicate these boundaries to others. By setting boundaries, individuals can create a sense of structure and control in their lives, which can help them to maintain a healthy balance between their various roles and responsibilities.

In addition to time management and setting boundaries, maintaining a healthy work-life balance is essential for balancing roles and responsibilities. This involves finding the right mix of work, family, and personal activities that allows individuals to feel fulfilled and content in all areas of their lives. It may involve making time for self-care activities, such as exercise, hobbies, or socializing, in order to recharge and prevent burnout. By prioritizing self-care and maintaining a healthy work-life balance, individuals can ensure that they are able to fulfill their various roles and responsibilities more effectively and sustainably.

It is also important for individuals to practice self-awareness and self-reflection in order to balance their roles and responsibilities effectively. By taking the time to reflect on their goals, values, and priorities, individuals can gain insight into what is most important to them and make informed decisions about how to allocate their time and energy. This may involve asking themselves questions such as: What are my long-term goals. What is most important to me in my personal and professional life. By examining these questions and taking the time to reflect on their answers, individuals can gain a deeper understanding of themselves and their motivations, which can help them to make more intentional choices about how to balance their roles and responsibilities. By taking a proactive and intentional approach to managing their various roles and responsibilities, individuals can ensure that they are able to fulfill their obligations without feeling overwhelmed or stressed. By prioritizing self-care and maintaining a healthy work-life balance, individuals can also improve their overall well-being and quality of life. Ultimately, by finding the right balance between their different roles and responsibilities, individuals can achieve greater success and fulfillment in all areas of their lives.

- Working together as a team

Working together as a team is a crucial aspect of achieving success in any organization. Whether in a business setting, a sports team, or a group project, collaboration and teamwork are essential for reaching goals and accomplishing tasks efficiently and effectively. By pooling together the diverse skills, perspectives, and experiences of team members, teams can achieve greater results than any individual could on their own.

One of the key benefits of working together as a team is the ability to leverage the unique strengths and talents of each team member. Each individual brings a different set of skills and capabilities to the table, and by working together, team members can complement each other and fill in each other's gaps. This allows tasks to be completed more quickly and with higher quality, as team members can focus on what they do best and rely on their colleagues to handle the rest. This division of labor and specialization can lead to increased productivity and efficiency, ultimately leading to better outcomes for the team as a whole.

In addition to leveraging individual strengths, working together as a team also allows for greater creativity and innovation. When individuals with diverse backgrounds and perspectives come together to solve a problem or tackle a challenge, they can generate a wider range of ideas and solutions than any one person could on their own. By encouraging open communication and collaboration, teams can spark creativity and innovation, leading to more effective problem-solving and decision-making. This creative synergy can lead to breakthrough ideas and solutions that may not have been possible without the input and collaboration of the entire team.

Furthermore, working together as a team can also foster a sense of camaraderie and mutual support among team members. By working towards a common goal and sharing in both the successes and challenges along the way, team members can build strong bonds and develop a sense of trust and unity. This sense of camaraderie can motivate team members to work harder and support each other, leading to a more positive and cohesive team dynamic. When team members feel supported and valued by their colleagues, they are more likely to be engaged and committed to the team's goals, leading to higher levels of performance and satisfaction.

However, working together as a team is not without its challenges. One of the key barriers to effective teamwork is communication, or the lack thereof. Poor communication can lead to misunderstandings, conflicts, and inefficiencies that can hinder the team's ability to work together effectively. It is essential for team members to practice active listening, provide clear and concise information, and ask for clarification when needed in order to ensure that all team members are on the same page and working towards the same goals.

Additionally, individual egos and conflicts can also pose challenges to working together as a team. When team members are more focused on promoting their own ideas and agendas rather than collaborating with their colleagues, it can create a toxic team environment that undermines trust and cooperation. It is essential for team members to set aside their egos and prioritize the team's overall goals and objectives in order to foster a positive and productive team dynamic. By recognizing and addressing individual conflicts and egos early on, teams can prevent these issues from escalating and work towards a more harmonious and effective working relationship. By leveraging the strengths and talents of each team member, fostering creativity and innovation, and building a sense of camaraderie and support among team members, teams can accomplish more together than any individual could on their own. While challenges such as poor communication and individual egos may arise, by prioritizing clear communication, active listening, and a focus on the team's goals, teams can overcome these obstacles and work towards a more collaborative and effective team dynamic. By working together as a team, organizations can harness the power of collective effort and achieve greater results than ever before.

Chapter 12: Finding Joy in Parenting

- Embracing the journey of parenthood

Parenthood is a transformative journey that many people embark on at some point in their lives. It is a journey filled with ups and downs, challenges and rewards, and a profound sense of love and responsibility. Embracing the journey of parenthood means accepting the unpredictability of raising a child and being open to the growth and change that comes with it. It requires patience, compassion, and a willingness to learn and adapt as you navigate the ever-evolving landscape of parenting.

One of the key aspects of embracing the journey of parenthood is recognizing that no two children are the same. Each child is a unique individual with their own strengths, weaknesses, and personality traits. As a parent, it is important to embrace and celebrate these differences, rather than trying to mold your child into someone they are not. By accepting and embracing your child for who they are, you can create a loving and supportive environment in which they can thrive and grow.

Another important aspect of embracing the journey of parenthood is understanding that parenting is a learning process. No one is born knowing how to be the perfect parent, and it is natural to make mistakes along the way. Instead of viewing these mistakes as failures, see them as opportunities for growth and development. By staying open to new ideas and approaches, seeking out support and resources, and being willing to reflect on your own parenting practices, you can continue to grow and evolve as a parent.

Parenting can be a challenging and demanding role, but it is also incredibly rewarding. Embracing the journey of parenthood means finding joy and fulfillment in the small moments of daily life with your child. Whether it's a shared laugh, a cozy snuggle, or a proud milestone moment, these little moments are what make the journey of parenthood so special. By cherishing these moments and staying present and engaged in your child's life, you can cultivate a deep and meaningful connection that will last a lifetime.

It is also important to remember that self-care is an essential part of embracing the journey of parenthood. Parenting can be all-consuming, and it is easy to put your own needs and well-being on the backburner in favor of taking care of your child. However, it is crucial to prioritize self-care and make time for yourself in order to be the best parent you can be. Whether it's carving out time for exercise, hobbies, or relaxation, taking care of your own physical, mental, and emotional well-being is essential for maintaining the energy and resilience needed to navigate the challenges of parenthood. By accepting and celebrating your child for who they are, embracing the learning process of parenting, finding joy in the small moments, prioritizing self-care, and staying present and engaged in your child's life, you can create a loving and nurturing environment in which both you and your child can flourish and thrive. Parenthood is a journey like no other, and by approaching it with an open heart and mind, you can experience the profound joys and rewards that come with raising a child.

- Celebrating milestones and achievements

Celebrating milestones and achievements is a crucial aspect of personal and professional growth. It allows individuals to reflect on their accomplishments, recognize their hard work and dedication, and provide motivation to continue striving for success. Whether it be landing a new job, completing a degree, starting a family, or reaching a fitness goal, celebrating these milestones helps reinforce a sense of accomplishment and satisfaction.

It is important to celebrate both small and large milestones in life. While major achievements such as graduating from college or landing a dream job may garner more attention, celebrating smaller milestones such as completing a project or reaching a personal goal is just as important. These smaller accomplishments are building blocks that lead to larger successes and should not be overlooked. By acknowledging and celebrating these smaller milestones, individuals can boost their confidence and motivation to continue moving forward.

Celebrating milestones and achievements not only benefits individuals on a personal level, but it also has a positive impact on their professional lives. Recognizing and celebrating achievements in the workplace can boost employee morale, motivation, and productivity. It can also foster a culture of appreciation and recognition, which can lead to increased job satisfaction and employee retention. By celebrating milestones and achievements, organizations can create a positive work environment that values and rewards hard work and success.

There are many ways to celebrate milestones and achievements, both personally and professionally. Some common ways include throwing a party or gathering with friends and family, treating oneself to a special meal or outing, or taking a moment to reflect and express gratitude for the accomplishment. In the workplace, celebrating milestones and achievements can involve recognizing employees at team meetings, hosting a luncheon or happy hour, or giving out awards or certificates. Regardless of the method, the important thing is to take the time to acknowledge and celebrate the hard work and dedication that led to the achievement.

While celebrating milestones and achievements is important, it is also essential to set new goals and continue striving for success. Celebrating achievements should not be seen as the end of the journey, but rather as a milestone on the path to continued growth and development. By setting new goals and challenges, individuals can maintain their momentum and drive towards further success. In this way, celebrating milestones becomes a way to recharge and refocus, rather than a final destination. It allows individuals to reflect on their accomplishments, recognize their hard work and dedication, and provide motivation to continue striving for success. By celebrating both small and large milestones, individuals can boost their confidence and motivation, create a positive work environment, and set themselves up for continued growth and success. So, take the time to acknowledge and celebrate your achievements, big and small, and keep moving forward towards your goals.

- Practicing self-care as a parent

Practicing self-care as a parent is crucial for maintaining a healthy balance between caring for your children and caring for yourself. It is easy for parents to neglect their own needs in favor of taking care of their children, but this ultimately leads to burnout and a diminished ability to effectively care for others. Self-care involves taking time for yourself, setting boundaries, and prioritizing your own physical and emotional well-being.

One of the most important aspects of self-care as a parent is taking time for yourself. This can be as simple as taking a few minutes each day to relax and unwind, or as indulgent as a weekend getaway. It is important to set aside time for activities that bring you joy and relaxation, whether that be reading a book, going for a walk, or enjoying a hobby. By taking time for yourself, you can recharge and come back to your parenting responsibilities with renewed energy and patience.

Setting boundaries is another critical component of self-care as a parent. It is important to establish boundaries with your children, partners, and other family members to ensure that your own needs are being met. This can include setting limits on how much time you spend on parenting duties, as well as clearly communicating your needs and expectations to others. By setting boundaries, you can prevent feelings of resentment and burnout, and ensure that you have the time and energy to care for yourself.

Prioritizing your physical and emotional well-being is also essential for practicing self-care as a parent. This can include making time for exercise, eating healthy meals, getting enough sleep, and seeking support when needed. It is easy for parents to neglect their own health in favor of caring for their children, but by prioritizing self-care, you can ensure that you are able to be present and engaged in your parenting role. Additionally, seeking support from friends, family, or a therapist can help you navigate the challenges of parenting and ensure that your own emotional needs are being met. By taking time for yourself, setting boundaries, and prioritizing your physical and emotional well-being, you can prevent burnout and ensure that you are able to be the best parent possible. Remember that self-care is not selfish, but necessary for maintaining your well-being and ability to effectively care for others. By investing in your own self-care, you are investing in the well-being of your entire family.

Chapter 13: Handling Transitions and Changes

- Adjusting to new family dynamics

Adjusting to new family dynamics can be a challenging and complex process that requires patience, understanding, and open communication. Whether a result of marriage, divorce, adoption, or other life changes, new family dynamics can bring about a range of emotions and adjustments for all involved. This transition period is a critical time for all family members to come together, support one another, and navigate through changes in roles, expectations, and routines.

One of the key factors in adjusting to new family dynamics is communication. Open and honest communication is essential for addressing any concerns, fears, or misunderstandings that may arise during this time of change. It is important for family members to express their feelings, listen to one another, and work together to find solutions to any challenges that may arise. This may involve family meetings, individual conversations, or even seeking the help of a therapist or counselor to facilitate healthy communication and problem-solving.

Another important aspect of adjusting to new family dynamics is establishing boundaries and expectations. As roles shift and relationships evolve, it is necessary for family members to set clear boundaries and expectations to ensure that everyone feels respected and understood. This may involve discussing new rules, routines, or responsibilities within the family, as well as outlining boundaries for privacy, personal space, and decision-making. By establishing clear boundaries and expectations, family members can avoid misunderstandings and conflicts, and create a more harmonious and supportive environment for everyone.

Flexibility is also key in adjusting to new family dynamics. As families change and grow, it is important to be flexible and adaptable to new situations and challenges that may arise. This may involve being open to new ideas, perspectives, and ways of doing things, as well as being willing to make adjustments and compromises for the well-being of the family as a whole. By practicing flexibility and adaptability, family members can navigate through changes in a positive and constructive way, and foster resilience and strength in the face of any obstacles that may come their way.

Support from extended family, friends, or other support networks can also be beneficial in adjusting to new family dynamics. Having a strong support system can provide comfort, guidance, and encouragement during this time of transition, and can help family members feel connected, understood, and valued. Whether it is through seeking advice, sharing experiences, or simply having someone to talk to, having a support system can make a big difference in helping family members adjust to new dynamics and navigate through challenges together. By fostering healthy communication, setting clear boundaries and expectations, practicing flexibility and adaptability, and seeking support from others, family members can navigate through changes in a positive and constructive way. It is important for families to come together, support one another, and work as a team to create a harmonious and supportive environment that allows everyone to thrive and grow. By working together and embracing change, families can strengthen their bonds, deepen their connections, and create a lasting foundation for a happy and healthy future.

- Coping with life changes

Life is full of changes, both big and small, that can sometimes feel overwhelming and unsettling. Whether it's starting a new job, moving to a new city, ending a relationship, or dealing with a loss, coping with life changes is an inevitable part of the human experience. It's important to remember that it's normal to feel a range of emotions when faced with change, including fear, sadness, excitement, and uncertainty. However, there are strategies that can help you navigate these transitions with grace and resilience.

One of the most important things to remember when coping with life changes is to give yourself permission to feel whatever emotions come up. It's natural to feel a mix of positive and negative emotions when faced with change, and trying to suppress or ignore these feelings can actually make the adjustment process more difficult. Instead, try to practice self-compassion and acceptance of your emotions, recognizing that they are a normal part of the human experience.

Another helpful strategy for coping with life changes is to practice self-care and prioritize your well-being. During times of transition, it's easy to neglect your own needs and focus solely on adapting to the new circumstances. However, taking care of yourself both physically and emotionally is crucial for navigating change in a healthy way. This can involve things like getting enough sleep, eating nutritious foods, exercising regularly, and engaging in activities that bring you joy and relaxation.

In addition to self-care, building a support network can also be instrumental in coping with life changes. Having a strong support system of friends, family, or even a therapist can provide you with the emotional support and guidance you need during times of transition. Talking about your feelings, seeking advice, and receiving validation from others can help you process your emotions and gain perspective on the changes you are facing. It's important to lean on your support system when needed and not be afraid to ask for help when you need it.

Another helpful strategy for coping with life changes is to practice mindfulness and stay present in the moment. When faced with uncertainty and upheaval, it's easy to get caught up in worrying about the future or dwelling on the past. However, practicing mindfulness can help you stay grounded and centered in the present moment, allowing you to better cope with the challenges of change. Simple practices like deep breathing, meditation, and staying engaged in the present moment can help you find a sense of calm and clarity during times of transition.

In closing, it's important to remember that change is a natural and inevitable part of life, and that with every change comes the opportunity for growth and transformation. While coping with life changes can be difficult and challenging, it can also be an opportunity for self-discovery, personal development, and new beginnings. By acknowledging your emotions, practicing self-care, building a support network, staying present in the moment, and embracing change as a catalyst for growth, you can navigate life's transitions with resilience and grace. Remember that you are not alone in facing change, and that with time and self-compassion, you can emerge stronger and more resilient on the other side.

- Supporting children through transitions

Transitions can be challenging for children as they navigate changes in their environment, routines, and relationships. As adults, it is important for us to support children through these transitions to help them feel secure and confident as they adjust to new circumstances. There are several strategies that can be employed to assist children during transitions, including providing clear communication, offering reassurance and stability, and fostering a sense of belonging and connection.

One of the key ways to support children through transitions is by providing clear and consistent communication. This can help children understand what to expect during the transition and alleviate any anxiety or uncertainty they may be feeling. By providing information about the upcoming changes and answering any questions they may have, we can help children feel more prepared and less overwhelmed by the transition. It is also important to communicate honestly with children, keeping them informed about any changes or developments as they arise.

In addition to clear communication, offering reassurance and stability can help children feel supported during transitions. Children often look to adults for guidance and reassurance during times of change, and it is important for us to provide them with a sense of security and stability. This can be achieved by maintaining consistent routines and rituals, such as mealtimes, bedtime routines, and daily activities. By keeping these familiar aspects of their lives in place, we can help children feel more secure and grounded as they navigate the transition.

Another important aspect of supporting children through transitions is fostering a sense of belonging and connection. Children thrive when they feel connected to others and part of a supportive community. During times of transition, it is important for us to provide children with opportunities to connect with others, whether it be through social interactions, group activities, or one-on-one time with a caring adult. By fostering a sense of belonging and connection, we can help children feel more supported and confident as they navigate the changes in their lives. By providing clear communication, offering reassurance and stability, and fostering a sense of belonging and connection, we can help children feel secure and confident as they navigate changes in their environment, routines, and relationships. As adults, it is our responsibility to support children through transitions and help them feel supported and empowered during times of change. By employing these strategies, we can help children thrive and succeed as they adapt to new circumstances and experiences.

Chapter 14: Embracing Diversity and Inclusion

- Celebrating differences

Celebrating differences is a concept that emphasizes the importance of embracing and valuing diversity in all its forms. It recognizes that each individual is unique and brings a different perspective, background, and set of experiences to the table. By celebrating these differences, we are able to foster a more inclusive and equitable society where everyone feels valued and respected.

One of the key aspects of celebrating differences is the recognition that diversity is a strength, not a weakness. When individuals from different backgrounds come together, they are able to bring a wealth of knowledge, skills, and abilities to the table. This diversity of thought and perspective can lead to more innovative solutions, better decision-making, and a more enriched community as a whole. By embracing and celebrating these differences, we can create a more dynamic and vibrant society where everyone has a role to play and a contribution to make.

Another important aspect of celebrating differences is the promotion of empathy and understanding. When we take the time to learn about and appreciate the experiences and perspectives of others, we are able to build stronger relationships and create a more united community. By listening to and respecting the viewpoints of others, we can develop a greater sense of empathy and compassion for those who may be different from us. This can lead to a more compassionate and empathetic society where everyone feels seen, heard, and valued.

Additionally, celebrating differences can help to combat discrimination and prejudice. By highlighting the unique qualities and contributions of individuals from diverse backgrounds, we can challenge stereotypes and misconceptions that may lead to discrimination. When we actively promote and celebrate diversity, we send a powerful message that everyone has value and deserves to be treated with respect and dignity. This can help to create a more inclusive and equitable society where all individuals are able to thrive and reach their full potential.

In order to truly celebrate differences, it is important to create spaces and opportunities for dialogue and engagement. This can involve organizing events and activities that bring individuals from diverse backgrounds together to share their experiences, learn from one another, and celebrate their unique identities. By creating these opportunities for interaction and collaboration, we can break down barriers, build connections, and create a more cohesive and united community. By embracing and valuing diversity, we can harness the unique strengths and perspectives of individuals from all backgrounds to create a more dynamic and vibrant community. Through empathy, understanding, and engagement, we can combat discrimination and prejudice and build a more united and harmonious society where everyone has the opportunity to thrive. Let us continue to celebrate our differences and work together to create a more inclusive and equitable world for all.

- Teaching tolerance and acceptance

Teaching tolerance and acceptance is a crucial aspect of promoting diversity and inclusion in today's society. In a world that is becoming increasingly interconnected, it is essential for individuals to have an understanding and appreciation for different cultures, beliefs, and perspectives. By fostering an environment of tolerance and acceptance, we can create a more harmonious and accepting community where everyone is valued and respected.

One of the key ways to teach tolerance and acceptance is through education. Schools play a fundamental role in shaping young minds and instilling values of empathy and understanding. Educators can incorporate lessons on diversity, inclusivity, and social justice into their curriculum to help students develop a broader perspective and a deeper appreciation for the world around them. By exposing students to different cultures, traditions, and viewpoints, they can learn to respect and celebrate the differences that make each individual unique.

Additionally, teaching tolerance and acceptance requires open and honest conversations about privilege, discrimination, and bias. By addressing these challenging topics head-on, educators can help students recognize and confront their own biases, as well as understand the impact of systemic inequality on marginalized communities. By creating a safe space for dialogue and reflection, educators can empower students to become advocates for social justice and equality in their own communities.

Furthermore, teaching tolerance and acceptance extends beyond the classroom and into everyday interactions. It is important for individuals to actively listen to others, seek to understand their perspectives, and show empathy for their experiences. By practicing kindness, respect, and compassion in our interactions with others, we can build a more inclusive and accepting society where everyone feels valued and respected. By fostering a culture of empathy, understanding, and respect, we can embrace diversity and celebrate the unique contributions of each individual. Through education, open dialogue, and everyday acts of kindness, we can cultivate a community where everyone is accepted and valued for who they are. Let us commit ourselves to teaching tolerance and acceptance in all aspects of our lives, and strive to create a world where diversity is celebrated and differences are embraced.

- Building a culturally inclusive environment

Building a culturally inclusive environment is crucial in today's diverse and interconnected world. In order to foster a sense of belonging and respect for all individuals, organizations must proactively work towards creating a culture that values diversity and promotes inclusivity. This involves not only celebrating different cultural backgrounds, but also ensuring that all individuals feel heard, respected, and valued for who they are.

One of the key components of building a culturally inclusive environment is recognizing and acknowledging the diversity of the people within an organization. This includes understanding that diversity goes beyond race and ethnicity to encompass a wide range of identities, such as gender, sexual orientation, religion, age, ability, and more. By recognizing and valuing this diversity, organizations can create an environment where all individuals feel accepted and respected for who they are.

Another important aspect of building a culturally inclusive environment is promoting cultural competence among staff members. Cultural competence involves having the knowledge, skills, and attitudes necessary to effectively interact with individuals from different cultural backgrounds. This includes being aware of one's own cultural biases, understanding the cultural norms and values of others, and being able to adapt one's behavior and communication style to be more inclusive and respectful of diverse perspectives.

In addition to promoting cultural competence, organizations must also work towards creating policies and practices that promote inclusivity and equity. This includes adopting non-discriminatory hiring practices, providing training on diversity and inclusion, and creating opportunities for all individuals to participate in decision-making processes. By creating a more inclusive and equitable workplace, organizations can ensure that all individuals have an equal opportunity to succeed and thrive.

One way to build a culturally inclusive environment is to actively listen to the needs and concerns of individuals from diverse backgrounds. This involves creating a safe space for open and honest communication, where individuals feel comfortable sharing their experiences and perspectives. By actively listening and responding to the needs of all individuals, organizations can create a more inclusive and supportive environment where everyone feels valued and respected.

Additionally, organizations can promote inclusivity by fostering a sense of belonging among all individuals. This can be done by creating opportunities for individuals to connect with others who share similar backgrounds or interests, as well as by celebrating the unique contributions that each individual brings to the organization. By fostering a sense of belonging, organizations can create a more positive and welcoming environment where all individuals feel valued and respected. By recognizing and valuing the diversity of individuals, promoting cultural competence among staff members, creating inclusive policies and practices, actively listening to the needs of individuals, and fostering a sense of belonging, organizations can create a more inclusive and equitable workplace where all individuals feel valued and respected. By taking these steps, organizations can create a culture that celebrates diversity and promotes inclusivity, leading to a more engaged and productive workforce.

Chapter 15: Teaching Life Skills

- Encouraging independence

Encouraging independence is a crucial aspect of human development that empowers individuals to take control of their lives and make decisions that align with their personal values and goals. It is a skill that is cultivated through various life experiences and interactions with others, and it plays a significant role in shaping a person's sense of self-efficacy and autonomy. Independence is not about doing everything on one's own, but rather about having the confidence and ability to navigate through life's challenges and make informed choices. It is about taking ownership of one's actions and responsibilities and not being overly reliant on others for guidance or validation.

One of the key factors that contribute to fostering independence in individuals is providing them with opportunities for growth and development. This can be achieved through a variety of means, such as encouraging them to try new things, pursue their interests, and take on new challenges. By exposing individuals to different tasks and experiences, they can build their skills and capabilities, which in turn boost their confidence and self-reliance. For example, parents can support their children in exploring different hobbies and interests, enrolling them in extracurricular activities, and encouraging them to take on leadership roles in school or community projects. Similarly, employers can provide their employees with training and development opportunities to enhance their skills and competencies, empowering them to take on more responsibilities in the workplace.

In addition to providing opportunities for growth, it is essential to foster a supportive environment that encourages independence. This involves creating a safe and nurturing space where individuals feel empowered to make decisions and take risks without fear of judgment or criticism. By offering positive reinforcement and constructive feedback, we can help individuals build their confidence and overcome challenges. For example, teachers can praise students for their efforts and progress, even if they make mistakes along the way. Similarly, managers can acknowledge their employees' contributions and provide them with constructive feedback to help them improve their performance. By creating a culture of support and encouragement, we can motivate individuals to strive for excellence and take initiative in their personal and professional lives.

Another important aspect of encouraging independence is promoting problem-solving and critical thinking skills. These skills are essential for individuals to navigate through life's complexities and uncertainties, enabling them to make informed decisions and overcome obstacles. By encouraging individuals to think critically and analyze situations from different perspectives, we can help them develop a greater sense of autonomy and self-reliance. This can be achieved through educational activities that promote problem-solving and decision-making skills, such as group projects, case studies, and real-world simulations. By challenging individuals to think outside the box and consider alternative solutions, we can empower them to become more independent in their thinking and decision-making processes.

Furthermore, fostering independence also involves promoting self-awareness and self-reflection in individuals. By encouraging individuals to explore their strengths, weaknesses, values, and beliefs, we can help them develop a better understanding of themselves and their goals. This self-awareness is essential for individuals to make informed choices that are aligned with their personal values and aspirations. For example, students can participate in self-assessment activities to identify their strengths and areas for improvement, allowing them to set realistic goals and track their progress over time. Similarly, professionals can engage in reflective practices, such as journaling or peer feedback, to gain insights into their performance and areas for growth. By promoting self-awareness and self-reflection, we can empower individuals to take ownership of their lives and make decisions that lead to personal fulfillment and success. By providing opportunities for growth, fostering a supportive environment, promoting problem-solving and critical thinking skills, and encouraging self-awareness and self-reflection, we can help individuals build their confidence and self-reliance. Ultimately, independence is not about doing everything on one's own, but rather about having the confidence and ability to navigate through life's challenges and make informed choices. By fostering independence in individuals, we can empower them to become more resilient, adaptable, and successful in their personal and professional lives.

- Teaching money management

Teaching money management is a crucial skill that individuals need in order to navigate the complex world of personal finance. Money management encompasses a variety of concepts, including budgeting, saving, investing, and spending wisely. By mastering these skills, individuals can achieve their financial goals and secure their financial futures. However, many people struggle with money management due to a lack of education and understanding. That's why it's important for educators and financial professionals to provide guidance and support in teaching money management.

One of the key components of teaching money management is helping individuals create a budget. A budget is a financial plan that outlines income and expenses, allowing individuals to track their spending and make informed financial decisions. By teaching individuals how to create a budget, educators can empower them to take control of their finances and make better choices with their money. Budgeting helps individuals prioritize their expenses, save for the future, and avoid unnecessary debt. In addition, budgeting can also help individuals identify areas where they can cut costs and save money.

Another important aspect of teaching money management is helping individuals understand the importance of saving. Saving is essential for building an emergency fund, investing for the future, and achieving long-term financial goals. By teaching individuals the benefits of saving and how to effectively save money, educators can help them secure their financial futures and avoid financial hardship. Saving requires discipline and commitment, but with the right guidance and support, individuals can develop healthy saving habits that will serve them well throughout their lives.

Investing is another key aspect of money management that individuals need to understand in order to build wealth and achieve financial success. Investing allows individuals to grow their money over time by putting it to work in the stock market, real estate, or other investment vehicles. By teaching individuals the basics of investing, educators can help them make informed investment decisions and build a diversified portfolio that aligns with their financial goals. Investing carries risks, but with proper guidance and knowledge, individuals can mitigate those risks and maximize their returns.

Teaching individuals how to spend wisely is also an important component of money management. Wise spending means making informed purchasing decisions, avoiding impulse buys, and living within one's means. By teaching individuals how to distinguish between needs and wants, educators can help them make conscious spending choices that align with their financial goals. Wise spending also involves comparison shopping, researching products and services, and looking for discounts and deals. By instilling these habits in individuals, educators can help them stretch their dollars further and make the most of their money. By providing education and guidance in budgeting, saving, investing, and spending wisely, educators can empower individuals to take control of their finances and make informed financial decisions. Money management is a lifelong skill that requires practice and dedication, but with the right support and knowledge, individuals can build a solid financial foundation that will serve them well throughout their lives. It's never too late to start learning about money management, and by investing in financial education, individuals can set themselves up for a prosperous and secure future.

- Developing problem-solving skills

Problem-solving skills are essential in both professional and personal settings. They help individuals to effectively analyze situations, identify potential solutions, and implement the best course of action. Developing these skills requires practice, patience, and a willingness to learn. In this article, we will explore the importance of problem-solving skills, discuss strategies for enhancing them, and provide tips for overcoming common obstacles.

One of the key reasons why problem-solving skills are so important is that they are transferable across various areas of life. Whether you are facing a complex work project, a personal dilemma, or a challenging academic task, the ability to think critically and creatively can help you navigate through obstacles with confidence. Employers also value employees who possess strong problem-solving skills, as they are often seen as proactive, resourceful, and reliable team members.

To enhance your problem-solving skills, it is important to first understand the stages of the problem-solving process. This typically involves identifying the issue, gathering relevant information, generating possible solutions, evaluating those solutions, and implementing the best one. By following these steps systematically, you can approach problems in a structured and methodical way, which can increase your chances of finding a successful resolution.

Another effective strategy for developing problem-solving skills is to practice mindfulness and self-awareness. This involves taking the time to reflect on your thoughts, emotions, and behaviors when faced with a problem. By being aware of your own cognitive biases and tendencies, you can make more informed decisions and avoid the pitfalls of automatic thinking. This self-reflection can also help you to identify areas for improvement and growth, which is essential for continuous learning and development.

In addition to self-awareness, collaboration and communication are also crucial for enhancing problem-solving skills. Working with others can provide different perspectives, insights, and solutions that you may not have considered on your own. By fostering a collaborative environment where team members feel comfortable sharing their ideas and feedback, you can leverage the collective expertise of the group to tackle complex problems more effectively.

It is important to note that developing problem-solving skills is a gradual process that requires patience and persistence. It is natural to encounter setbacks and challenges along the way, but it is important to view these obstacles as learning opportunities rather than failures. By reframing your mindset and adopting a growth-oriented approach, you can cultivate resilience and adaptability, which are essential qualities for effective problem solvers. By following the strategies outlined in this article, you can enhance your problem-solving abilities and become a more effective problem solver in both professional and personal settings. Remember to approach problems with an open mind, a collaborative spirit, and a willingness to learn from experience. With practice and dedication, you can develop the problem-solving skills needed to thrive in an ever-changing and complex world.

Chapter 16: Balancing Discipline and Love

- Setting boundaries with love

Setting boundaries with love is an essential component of maintaining healthy relationships and ensuring personal well-being. Boundaries are the invisible lines that define the limits of acceptable behavior in a relationship, and they serve as a protective barrier against emotional harm and manipulation. When boundaries are not clearly defined or enforced, individuals run the risk of feeling overwhelmed, exploited, or disrespected in their interactions with others. Therefore, it is crucial to establish and maintain boundaries in all relationships, whether they be romantic, familial, or platonic.

The concept of setting boundaries with love entails the notion of asserting one's needs and limits in a respectful and compassionate manner. It involves communicating clearly and assertively with others about what is and is not acceptable behavior, and being willing to enforce consequences when boundaries are violated. Setting boundaries with love also involves acknowledging and validating the feelings and needs of others while prioritizing one's own self-care and well-being. This approach allows individuals to assert their boundaries without coming across as hostile or aggressive, fostering mutual understanding and respect in relationships.

One of the key aspects of setting boundaries with love is self-awareness. Before you can effectively communicate your boundaries to others, you must first be aware of your own needs, limits, and values. Reflect on what behaviors or interactions make you feel uncomfortable, stressed, or disrespected, and consider how you can assert your boundaries in those situations. It is also important to recognize that your boundaries may evolve over time, so it is essential to regularly check in with yourself and reassess your boundaries as needed.

Once you have a clear understanding of your own boundaries, the next step is to communicate them effectively to others. This can be challenging, especially if you are not used to asserting yourself in relationships. However, setting boundaries is a skill that can be developed with practice. Start by expressing your boundaries in a calm and assertive manner, using "I" statements to communicate how you feel and what you need. For example, instead of saying, "You always interrupt me when I'm speaking," try saying, "I feel disrespected when I am interrupted while talking. I would appreciate it if you could let me finish before responding. "

It is also essential to be consistent in enforcing your boundaries. When someone crosses a boundary, calmly but firmly remind them of your limits and consequences for violating them. Remember that setting boundaries is not about controlling others or punishing them but about taking care of yourself and ensuring healthy and respectful relationships. Be prepared for resistance or pushback from others, as not everyone may be receptive to your boundaries initially. Stay firm in your convictions and remind yourself that you deserve to be treated with respect and dignity.

In addition to communicating and enforcing your boundaries with others, it is crucial to take care of yourself and prioritize self-care. Setting boundaries with love also means setting boundaries with yourself and honoring your own needs and well-being. Make time for activities that bring you joy and relaxation, practice self-care rituals such as meditation or exercise, and seek support from friends, family, or a therapist when needed. Remember that setting boundaries is an act of self-love and self-respect, and it is essential for maintaining your emotional and mental health in relationships. By being self-aware, communicating effectively, and enforcing boundaries consistently, individuals can assert their needs and limits while fostering understanding and respect in their relationships. Remember that setting boundaries is an act of self-love and self-care, and it is essential for protecting your emotional well-being and maintaining healthy connections with others. Approach setting boundaries with love as a way to honor yourself and your relationships, and you will create a more fulfilling and harmonious life for yourself and those around you.

- Maintaining a positive parent-child relationship

Maintaining a positive parent-child relationship is crucial for the healthy development and well-being of both the parent and the child. It is a dynamic and evolving relationship that requires effort and commitment from both parties. In order to foster a positive parent-child relationship, it is important for parents to create a supportive and nurturing environment in which their child can thrive. This involves being attuned to their child's needs, emotions, and interests, and being responsive to their cues and signals.

One of the key elements of maintaining a positive parent-child relationship is effective communication. It is essential for parents to communicate openly and honestly with their child, and to listen attentively to their child's thoughts, feelings, and concerns. By fostering open and honest communication, parents can create a safe and trusting environment in which their child feels comfortable expressing themselves and sharing their thoughts and emotions.

Another important aspect of maintaining a positive parent-child relationship is setting clear and consistent boundaries. Boundaries help children feel safe and secure, and provide them with a sense of structure and predictability. It is important for parents to establish age-appropriate rules and expectations, and to enforce them in a fair and consistent manner. By setting and enforcing boundaries, parents can help their child develop self-discipline, responsibility, and respect for authority.

Building a strong emotional connection with their child is also essential for maintaining a positive parent-child relationship. Parents can strengthen their emotional bond with their child by spending quality time together, engaging in meaningful activities, and showing affection and support. By being emotionally available and responsive to their child's needs, parents can create a secure attachment that fosters a sense of trust, security, and belonging.

In addition to fostering open communication, setting clear boundaries, and building a strong emotional connection, parents can also promote a positive parent-child relationship by being supportive and encouraging. It is important for parents to provide their child with love, encouragement, and praise, and to show appreciation for their efforts and accomplishments. By being supportive and encouraging, parents can boost their child's self-esteem, confidence, and sense of competence, and help them develop a positive self-image.

Maintaining a positive parent-child relationship also involves resolving conflicts and disagreements in a constructive and respectful manner. Conflict is a natural and inevitable part of any relationship, and it is important for parents to model healthy conflict resolution skills for their child. Parents can teach their child how to express their thoughts and feelings assertively, how to listen actively and empathetically, and how to negotiate and compromise effectively. By modeling and teaching their child healthy conflict resolution skills, parents can help their child develop the ability to resolve conflicts in a positive and respectful way.

All in all, maintaining a positive parent-child relationship requires ongoing effort and commitment from both parties. It is important for parents to be patient, flexible, and understanding, and to approach their relationship with their child with an open mind and a willingness to learn and grow. By investing time, energy, and attention in their relationship with their child, parents can create a strong and enduring bond that will support their child's development, well-being, and success throughout their lives. By fostering open communication, setting clear boundaries, building a strong emotional connection, being supportive and encouraging, resolving conflicts constructively, and committing to ongoing effort and growth, parents can create a nurturing and supportive environment in which their child can thrive. By investing in their relationship with their child, parents can help their child develop the skills, values, and qualities they need to navigate life's challenges, build healthy relationships, and achieve their full potential.

- Balancing discipline with nurturing

Balancing discipline with nurturing is a crucial aspect of effective parenting and education. Discipline is often seen as the enforcement of rules and regulations, while nurturing involves providing care, support, and encouragement. Finding the right balance between these two elements is essential for fostering healthy development in children and students.

One key aspect of balancing discipline with nurturing is setting clear expectations and boundaries. Discipline involves establishing rules and consequences for inappropriate behavior, while nurturing involves providing positive reinforcement for good behavior. By clearly communicating expectations and boundaries, parents and educators can help children understand what is expected of them and why certain behaviors are not acceptable.

At the same time, it is important to approach discipline with empathy and understanding. Rather than resorting to harsh punishments, parents and educators should strive to understand the underlying reasons for a child's behavior and address any underlying issues that may be contributing to it. By approaching discipline with empathy and understanding, adults can help children learn from their mistakes and make positive changes in their behavior.

In addition to setting clear expectations and boundaries, it is also important to provide children and students with opportunities for growth and development. Nurturing involves supporting children's interests, talents, and passions, and providing them with opportunities to explore and develop their skills. By nurturing children's interests and talents, parents and educators can help them build confidence, self-esteem, and a sense of achievement.

Furthermore, it is important to be consistent in both discipline and nurturing. Consistency helps children and students understand what is expected of them and reinforces the importance of following rules and regulations. By being consistent in their approach to discipline and nurturing, parents and educators can create a stable and predictable environment that promotes healthy development in children and students. By setting clear expectations and boundaries, approaching discipline with empathy and understanding, providing opportunities for growth and development, and being consistent in their approach, parents and educators can create a supportive and nurturing environment that promotes positive behavior and healthy development.

Ultimately, finding the right balance between discipline and nurturing is key to raising happy, confident, and well-adjusted children and students.

86

Chapter 17: Growing Together as a Family

- Creating traditions and rituals

Traditions and rituals play a significant role in shaping the culture and identity of a group of people. They serve as a way to pass down values, beliefs, and practices from one generation to the next, creating a sense of continuity and connection between individuals. Traditions and rituals can be found in various aspects of society, ranging from religious ceremonies and family celebrations to cultural festivals and national holidays. In this essay, we will explore the importance of creating traditions and rituals, how they are formed, and their impact on individuals and communities.

Creating traditions and rituals is a process that involves the repetition of certain actions, behaviors, or activities over time. These repeated actions become meaningful and significant to individuals and groups, often symbolizing important events, beliefs, or values. For example, a family may have a tradition of gathering for dinner every Sunday night, which serves as a way to bond and connect with one another. Likewise, a religious community may have rituals such as prayer services or ceremonies that are performed regularly to express devotion and reverence.

One of the key reasons for creating traditions and rituals is to provide a sense of stability and continuity in an ever-changing world. In a rapidly evolving society, traditions and rituals serve as anchor points that help individuals feel grounded and connected to their past. They provide a sense of comfort and familiarity, allowing people to feel a sense of belonging and identity. For example, a community that celebrates a cultural festival every year may feel a strong sense of pride and unity in coming together to honor their shared heritage and customs.

Traditions and rituals also serve as a way to transmit values and beliefs from one generation to the next. Through the practice of certain rituals and traditions, individuals learn about the customs, norms, and beliefs of their community. They are able to understand and appreciate the history and heritage of their culture, as well as the values that are important to their community. For example, a family that celebrates a particular holiday each year may pass down stories and rituals to their children, teaching them about the significance of the holiday and the values it represents.

In addition to providing a sense of stability and continuity, traditions and rituals also play a role in creating a sense of community and connection among individuals. By participating in shared traditions and rituals, individuals are able to bond with one another and strengthen their relationships. Whether it is through participating in religious ceremonies, cultural festivals, or family celebrations, traditions and rituals provide opportunities for people to come together, celebrate their commonalities, and create lasting memories. These shared experiences help to forge strong bonds among individuals and foster a sense of unity and belonging within a community.

It is important to note that traditions and rituals are not fixed and unchanging, but rather evolve and adapt over time to reflect the changing needs and values of a society. As societies grow and change, so too do the traditions and rituals that shape their culture. In order for traditions and rituals to remain relevant and meaningful, it is important for individuals and communities to continue to create new traditions and rituals that reflect their values and beliefs. This may involve incorporating new practices, customs, and celebrations into existing traditions, or even creating entirely new rituals to mark important events and milestones. Traditions and rituals help to provide a sense of stability and continuity, transmit values and beliefs across generations, and create a sense of community and connection among individuals. By participating in shared traditions and rituals, individuals are able to bond with one another, strengthen their relationships, and forge a sense of unity and belonging within their community. As societies continue to evolve and change, it is important for individuals and communities to continue to create new traditions and rituals that reflect their values and beliefs, ensuring that these important cultural practices remain relevant and meaningful for generations to come.

- Spending quality time together

Spending quality time together is essential for building strong relationships and fostering a sense of connection within a family, friendship, or romantic partnership. Quality time can be defined as any time spent in meaningful and engaging activities that allow individuals to bond, communicate, and create lasting memories together. Whether it's having a deep conversation, going on a fun outing, or simply enjoying each other's company in a relaxed setting, the key is to prioritize each other's presence and undivided attention during this time.

Quality time is crucial for maintaining healthy and happy relationships, as it allows individuals to truly connect and engage with one another on a deeper level. In today's fast-paced and technology-driven world, it can be easy to get caught up in the busyness of daily life and neglect the importance of spending quality time with loved ones. However, taking the time to prioritize and schedule quality time together can have numerous benefits for both parties involved.

One of the main benefits of spending quality time together is the opportunity it provides for building trust and intimacy within a relationship. When individuals make a conscious effort to set aside time to focus solely on each other, they create a safe space for open and honest communication. This can help strengthen the bond between them and foster a sense of mutual understanding and respect. Quality time also allows for a deeper connection to be formed, as individuals have the chance to share their thoughts, feelings, and experiences in a meaningful way.

In addition to building trust and intimacy, spending quality time together can also help increase feelings of happiness and satisfaction within a relationship. When individuals feel connected and valued by their loved ones, they are more likely to experience positive emotions and a sense of fulfillment. Quality time provides the opportunity for individuals to relax, have fun, and enjoy each other's company, which can help reduce stress and improve overall well-being. By prioritizing quality time together, individuals can create lasting memories and strengthen their emotional bond, leading to a more fulfilling and rewarding relationship.

Furthermore, spending quality time together can help individuals develop a sense of teamwork and collaboration within their relationship. By engaging in activities together, individuals can learn to communicate effectively, problem-solve, and work towards common goals. This can promote a sense of unity and partnership, as individuals learn to support and encourage each other in their endeavors. Quality time can also help individuals develop a sense of empathy and understanding towards their partner, as they work together to navigate challenges and celebrate successes. By prioritizing time to connect, communicate, and create lasting memories together, individuals can foster trust, intimacy, and happiness within their relationships. Quality time provides the opportunity to relax, have fun, and strengthen emotional bonds, leading to a more fulfilling and rewarding connection. By making an effort to schedule and prioritize quality time together, individuals can build a sense of teamwork and collaboration, fostering a deeper sense of unity and partnership within their relationship. Ultimately, quality time is a valuable investment in a relationship, providing countless benefits for both parties involved.

- Building a strong family bond

Building a strong family bond is essential for the well-being and happiness of all family members. A strong family bond creates a sense of belonging, love, support, and security within the family unit. When family members feel connected and supported by one another, they are more likely to have better mental health, stronger relationships, and overall higher levels of life satisfaction.

One of the most important ways to build a strong family bond is through effective communication. Communication is key in any relationship, but it is particularly critical in family relationships. Family members should make an effort to listen to one another, express their feelings and thoughts openly, and communicate their needs and desires. By engaging in open and honest communication, family members can better understand each other, resolve conflicts, and strengthen their relationships.

Another important factor in building a strong family bond is spending quality time together. Quality time can take many forms, such as sharing meals, playing games, going on family outings, or simply spending time talking and connecting with one another. By making time for each other and engaging in activities that promote bonding, family members can create lasting memories and deepen their connections with one another.

In addition to communication and quality time, building a strong family bond also involves showing love and support for one another. Expressing love and appreciation for family members, offering emotional support in times of need, and encouraging each other to pursue their goals and dreams are all ways to strengthen the family bond. When family members feel loved, supported, and valued by one another, they are more likely to feel connected and secure in their relationships.

It is also important for families to establish and maintain traditions and rituals that promote unity and togetherness. Traditions can be as simple as celebrating birthdays, holidays, or family milestones, or they can be more elaborate, such as annual family vacations or reunions. By participating in traditions and rituals together, family members can create shared experiences and memories that strengthen their bonds and create a sense of continuity and belonging within the family unit.

Furthermore, building a strong family bond involves promoting respect, empathy, and understanding among family members. Respecting each other's opinions, boundaries, and differences, showing empathy and understanding in times of conflict or disagreement, and being willing to compromise and work towards common goals are all important aspects of building a strong family bond. When family members treat each other with respect and kindness, they are more likely to feel connected and valued within the family unit. By engaging in effective communication, spending quality time together, showing love and support, establishing traditions and rituals, and promoting respect, empathy, and understanding, families can strengthen their relationships and create lasting bonds that will endure through good times and bad. Family bonds are a source of strength, support, and comfort, and investing time and effort into building and maintaining these bonds is key to creating a happy and healthy family unit.

Chapter 18: Practicing Mindful Parenting

- Being present and engaged with your child

Being present and engaged with your child is a crucial aspect of parenting that can have a significant impact on their overall well-being and development. As parents, it is important to prioritize quality time with our children and to be fully present during these moments. This means putting aside distractions such as electronic devices and focusing on actively engaging with our children. Research has shown that children who have parents who are present and engaged in their lives tend to have higher self-esteem, better social skills, and improved academic performance.

One of the key ways to be present and engaged with your child is through active listening. This means truly paying attention to what your child is saying without being distracted or interrupting. By listening to your child with empathy and understanding, you are showing them that their thoughts and feelings are important to you. This can help strengthen your bond with your child and build trust between the two of you. Active listening also allows you to better understand your child's perspective and experiences, which can help you provide the support and guidance they need.

In addition to active listening, being present and engaged with your child involves spending quality time together. This could involve participating in activities that your child enjoys, such as playing sports, doing arts and crafts, or simply having a conversation. By actively participating in these activities with your child, you are showing them that you value their interests and enjoy spending time with them. Quality time together also provides opportunities for you to bond with your child, create lasting memories, and strengthen your relationship.

Another important aspect of being present and engaged with your child is being emotionally available. This means being responsive to your child's emotions and providing them with the support and comfort they need. Children look to their parents for emotional support and guidance, and being emotionally available allows you to meet their needs in a nurturing and caring way. By validating your child's emotions and offering them reassurance and encouragement, you are helping them feel secure and loved. This can have a positive impact on their emotional well-being and overall development.

It is also important to be consistent in your presence and engagement with your child. Children thrive on routine and predictability, and having consistent quality time with your child can help create a sense of security and stability for them. By making an effort to prioritize and schedule time for your child on a regular basis, you are showing them that they are a priority in your life. Consistency in your presence and engagement also allows you to build a strong and lasting connection with your child, which can have long-term benefits for their development and well-being. By actively listening, spending quality time together, being emotionally available, and being consistent in your presence and engagement, you can create a strong bond with your child and provide them with the support and guidance they need to thrive. Remember that being present and engaged with your child is not only beneficial for them, but for you as well. The time spent with your child can create cherished memories and strengthen the parent-child relationship, enriching both of your lives in the process.

- Managing stress and emotions

Managing stress and emotions is a critical aspect of maintaining overall well-being and mental health. In today's fast-paced and often overwhelming world, it is common for individuals to experience high levels of stress and a wide range of emotions on a daily basis. While some level of stress is normal and can even be beneficial in certain situations, chronic stress and unmanaged emotions can have detrimental effects on both physical and mental health. Therefore, it is crucial for individuals to develop effective strategies for managing stress and emotions in order to live a balanced and fulfilling life.

One of the key components of managing stress and emotions is developing self-awareness. Self-awareness involves recognizing one's own thoughts, feelings, and behaviors and understanding how they impact one's overall well-being. By being aware of our internal experiences, we can better identify the sources of our stress and negative emotions and take steps to address them. This may involve keeping a journal to track our thoughts and emotions, engaging in mindfulness practices such as meditation or deep breathing exercises, or seeking support from a therapist or counselor. Developing self-awareness also allows us to better understand our triggers and patterns of behavior, helping us to make more informed choices in how we respond to stress and emotions.

Another important aspect of managing stress and emotions is developing healthy coping mechanisms. When faced with stress or strong emotions, it can be tempting to engage in unhealthy behaviors such as overeating, substance abuse, or avoidance. However, these coping mechanisms only provide temporary relief and can ultimately worsen our mental health in the long run. Instead, it is important to develop healthy coping strategies that help us effectively manage stress and regulate our emotions. This may involve engaging in regular exercise, practicing relaxation techniques such as yoga or Tai Chi, engaging in creative activities such as painting or writing, or connecting with others through social support networks. By developing healthy coping mechanisms, we can build resilience and better manage the challenges that life throws our way.

In addition to self-awareness and healthy coping mechanisms, it is also important to cultivate a positive mindset in order to manage stress and emotions effectively. Our thoughts have a powerful impact on our emotions and behavior, so it is essential to challenge negative thought patterns and cultivate a more positive outlook on life. This may involve practicing gratitude by focusing on the things we are thankful for, reframing negative situations in a more positive light, or engaging in positive self-talk to boost our confidence and self-esteem. By cultivating a positive mindset, we can reduce our levels of stress and anxiety, improve our emotional well-being, and enhance our overall quality of life.

In brief, it is important to remember that managing stress and emotions is an ongoing process that requires practice and commitment. It is unrealistic to expect ourselves to be stress-free and emotionally balanced at all times, as stress is a natural part of life and emotions are constantly changing. Instead, we should focus on developing healthy habits and strategies that help us navigate the ups and downs of life more effectively. By prioritizing self-care, seeking support when needed, and remaining open to new coping mechanisms, we can build the resilience and emotional intelligence needed to manage stress and emotions in a healthy and sustainable way. By developing self-awareness, healthy coping mechanisms, a positive mindset, and a commitment to ongoing practice, individuals can effectively manage stress and regulate their emotions in a way that promotes overall well-being and fulfillment. It is important to remember that managing stress and emotions is a lifelong journey, and that it is okay to seek support from others when needed. By prioritizing self-care and staying proactive in our efforts to manage stress and emotions, we can lead happier, more balanced lives.

- Cultivating a mindful lifestyle

In today's fast-paced and hectic world, it can be easy to get caught up in the hustle and bustle of everyday life. However, cultivating a mindful lifestyle can help us slow down, be more present in the moment, and bring a sense of calm and clarity to our lives. Mindfulness is the practice of paying attention to the present moment without judgment, and it has been shown to have numerous benefits for our mental and physical health.

One of the key components of cultivating a mindful lifestyle is being aware of our thoughts and emotions. Often, we can get swept up in our thoughts and feelings, reacting automatically without taking the time to pause and reflect. By practicing mindfulness, we can learn to observe our thoughts and emotions without getting caught up in them. This can help us create space between our thoughts and our reactions, allowing us to respond more thoughtfully and intentionally in various situations.

Another important aspect of cultivating a mindful lifestyle is being present in the moment. In today's hyper-connected world, it can be easy to get distracted by technology, social media, and the constant barrage of information. However, by focusing on the present moment, we can engage more fully with our surroundings and the people around us. This can help us appreciate the beauty of everyday life and find joy in simple moments.

Practicing mindfulness also involves being kind and compassionate towards ourselves and others. Self-compassion is the practice of treating ourselves with the same kindness and understanding that we would offer to a close friend. By being kind to ourselves, we can cultivate a sense of inner peace and self-acceptance. Additionally, showing compassion towards others can help us build stronger relationships and foster a sense of connection and community.

In addition to the benefits for mental health, cultivating a mindful lifestyle can also have positive effects on our physical health. Mindfulness practices, such as meditation and deep breathing exercises, have been shown to reduce stress, lower blood pressure, and improve sleep quality. Whether through meditation, yoga, or simply taking a few moments each day to pause and breathe, there are many ways to incorporate mindfulness into our daily lives. By making a conscious effort to cultivate mindfulness, we can create a more peaceful, balanced, and fulfilling existence for ourselves and those around us.

Chapter 19: Building Resilience in Children

- Teaching coping skills

Teaching coping skills is a crucial aspect of mental health education and promotion that can greatly benefit individuals in managing stress, anxiety, and other challenging emotions. Coping skills are the strategies and techniques that individuals use to deal with difficult situations and emotions in a healthy and effective manner. By teaching coping skills, educators and mental health professionals can empower individuals to better navigate the ups and downs of life and build resilience in the face of adversity.

One of the key components of teaching coping skills is helping individuals identify their own unique triggers and stressors. Everyone experiences stress and difficult emotions differently, so it is important for individuals to understand what specific situations or thoughts tend to trigger their stress responses. By helping individuals become more aware of their triggers, educators and mental health professionals can assist them in developing personalized coping strategies that are tailored to their individual needs.

Once individuals have identified their triggers, the next step in teaching coping skills is helping them develop a toolbox of coping strategies that they can utilize when faced with difficult situations or emotions. Coping strategies can range from simple techniques like deep breathing and visualization to more complex skills like cognitive restructuring and problem-solving. By providing individuals with a range of coping strategies to choose from, educators and mental health professionals can empower them to find the techniques that work best for them in different situations.

In addition to teaching specific coping strategies, it is also important to educate individuals about the importance of self-care and self-compassion in managing stress and difficult emotions. Self-care involves taking care of one's physical, emotional, and mental well-being through activities like exercise, relaxation, and social connection. By emphasizing the importance of self-care, educators and mental health professionals can help individuals build a strong foundation for coping with stress and difficult emotions.

Another important aspect of teaching coping skills is helping individuals cultivate a growth mindset and resilience in the face of adversity. A growth mindset is the belief that challenges and setbacks can be opportunities for growth and learning, rather than insurmountable obstacles. By fostering a growth mindset in individuals, educators and mental health professionals can help them develop resilience and adaptability in the face of stress and difficult emotions. By helping individuals identify their triggers, develop a toolbox of coping strategies, prioritize self-care, and cultivate a growth mindset, educators and mental health professionals can empower individuals to navigate the ups and downs of life with resilience and confidence. By providing individuals with the skills and knowledge they need to cope effectively with stress and difficult emotions, we can help them lead healthier, more fulfilling lives.

- Encouraging perseverance

Perseverance is a key characteristic that can lead to success in various aspects of life. It is the ability to persist in the face of challenges, setbacks, and obstacles, and to continue working towards a goal despite the difficulties that may arise. Encouraging perseverance in individuals is important for helping them achieve their full potential and reach their goals. This can be especially crucial in academic and professional settings, where the journey to success is often filled with hurdles that require determination and resilience to overcome.

One way to encourage perseverance in individuals is to cultivate a growth mindset. This mindset is based on the belief that abilities can be developed through hard work, dedication, and effort. By fostering a growth mindset in individuals, they are more likely to view setbacks as opportunities for growth and learning, rather than as failures. This can help them stay motivated and continue working towards their goals, even when faced with challenges.

Providing support and encouragement is another effective way to promote perseverance in individuals. Whether it is through offering words of encouragement, providing guidance and advice, or simply being a listening ear, having a support system can make a significant difference in helping individuals stay motivated and resilient in the face of obstacles. By creating a supportive environment, individuals are more likely to feel empowered to persevere and continue working towards their goals.

Setting achievable goals and breaking them down into smaller, manageable steps can also help individuals stay motivated and persevere. By setting clear, specific goals, individuals can track their progress and celebrate their achievements along the way. Breaking down larger goals into smaller tasks can help make the journey towards success more manageable and less overwhelming. This can also help individuals stay focused and motivated, as they can see tangible progress towards their goals.

It is important to celebrate the small victories along the way and acknowledge the effort and hard work that individuals put in towards their goals. By recognizing and celebrating achievements, no matter how small, individuals are more likely to stay motivated and continue working towards their goals. This can help boost their self-confidence and reinforce the belief that perseverance and hard work are rewarded.

Providing opportunities for individuals to learn from their mistakes and failures can also help promote perseverance. By encouraging individuals to reflect on their setbacks and identify areas for improvement, they can develop a growth mindset and view failures as valuable learning experiences. This can help individuals build resilience and perseverance, as they are better equipped to handle challenges and setbacks in the future. By fostering a growth mindset, providing support and encouragement, setting achievable goals, celebrating achievements, and learning from mistakes, individuals can develop the resilience and determination needed to overcome obstacles and stay motivated on their path to success. By promoting perseverance in individuals, we can help them cultivate the skills and mindset needed to thrive in academic and professional settings, and ultimately achieve their goals.

- Helping children bounce back from setbacks

Children face setbacks and challenges on a regular basis as they navigate the complexities of growing up and learning about the world around them. Whether it's a disappointing grade on a test, a conflict with a friend, or a failure to meet a personal goal, setbacks can be difficult for children to process and overcome. However, it's important for parents, teachers, and caregivers to support children in bouncing back from these setbacks and developing the resilience they need to thrive in the face of adversity.

One key way to help children bounce back from setbacks is to encourage a growth mindset. In her research, psychologist Carol Dweck has emphasized the importance of teaching children that their abilities and intelligence are not fixed traits, but can be developed through effort and perseverance. By praising children for their effort rather than their innate abilities, we can help them build a belief in their own capacity for growth and improvement. When children encounter setbacks, they are more likely to see them as opportunities for learning and growth, rather than evidence of their limitations.

Another important aspect of helping children bounce back from setbacks is providing them with the support they need to process and make sense of their experiences. This may involve listening to children's feelings and thoughts without judgment, helping them identify and express their emotions, and offering guidance and perspective when needed. By creating a safe and supportive environment for children to navigate their setbacks, we can help them develop the emotional intelligence and coping skills they need to navigate life's challenges.

It's also important to help children develop a sense of resilience by teaching them problem-solving and coping skills. This may involve breaking down tasks into manageable steps, setting realistic goals, and helping children develop strategies for overcoming obstacles. By empowering children to take control of their own challenges and setbacks, we can help them build confidence in their ability to overcome adversity and bounce back stronger than before.

In addition to developing resilience in children, it's important to foster a sense of connection and belonging. Research has shown that children who feel connected to others and supported by their communities are more likely to bounce back from setbacks and thrive in the face of adversity. By building strong and supportive relationships with children, we can provide them with the emotional and social resources they need to navigate setbacks and challenges with confidence and resilience.

To wrap up, it's important to model resilience for children by showing them how to bounce back from our own setbacks and failures. By demonstrating perseverance, problem-solving, and emotional regulation in our own lives, we can teach children valuable lessons about resilience and empower them to overcome their own challenges. By serving as positive role models for children, we can inspire them to develop the skills and mindset they need to bounce back from setbacks and thrive in the face of adversity. By fostering a growth mindset, providing emotional support, teaching problem-solving and coping skills, fostering connections and belonging, and modeling resilience in our own lives, we can empower children to overcome setbacks and build the resilience they need to thrive in an ever-changing world. By working together to support and uplift the next generation, we can help children become confident, capable, and resilient individuals who are well-equipped to face life's challenges with courage and grace.

Chapter 20: Conclusion

- Recap of key strategies

In today's fast-paced and ever-changing business landscape, it is essential for organizations to have a clear understanding of key strategies in order to stay competitive and achieve success. In this recap, we will delve into some of the fundamental strategies that can help businesses thrive in a dynamic environment.

One of the most important strategies for any organization is to have a clear and well-defined vision and mission statement. This serves as the guiding force for the company, shaping its goals and objectives. A strong vision statement helps to align the efforts of employees towards a common purpose, while a mission statement outlines the specific actions and strategies that will be taken to achieve these goals. By having a clear vision and mission, organizations can stay focused on their long-term goals and navigate challenges with a sense of purpose.

Another key strategy that businesses must adopt is effective communication. Communication plays a crucial role in ensuring that all stakeholders are on the same page and working towards the same goals. This includes internal communication among employees, as well as external communication with customers, suppliers, and other partners. By fostering open and transparent communication channels, organizations can avoid misunderstandings, foster collaboration, and build strong relationships with stakeholders.

In addition to communication, organizations must also focus on fostering a culture of continuous learning and innovation. With technology evolving at a rapid pace and customer preferences constantly changing, businesses must be agile and adaptable in order to remain competitive. This means encouraging employees to constantly seek new knowledge and skills, as well as promoting a culture of experimentation and innovation. By embracing change and encouraging a growth mindset, organizations can stay ahead of the curve and identify new opportunities for growth.

One of the key strategies that businesses must implement to stay competitive in today's market is a strong focus on customer experience. In a world where consumers have more choices than ever before, businesses must prioritize delivering exceptional customer service and creating memorable experiences for their customers. This includes understanding customer needs and preferences, providing personalized solutions, and going above and beyond to exceed customer expectations. By placing the customer at the center of their operations, organizations can build strong relationships, drive loyalty, and differentiate themselves from competitors.

Lastly, organizations must also prioritize sustainability and social responsibility as key strategies for long-term success. In today's environmentally conscious world, consumers are increasingly looking for businesses that are committed to making a positive impact on society and the planet. By adopting sustainable practices, reducing their carbon footprint, and giving back to the community, organizations can attract socially responsible consumers, enhance their reputation, and contribute to a better world. By integrating sustainability and social responsibility into their core business practices, organizations can create shared value for both their stakeholders and society as a whole. By staying true to their core values and focusing on the needs of their stakeholders, businesses can build a strong foundation for growth and achieve sustainable competitive advantage.

- Encouragement for parents

Parenting is a challenging role that comes with its own set of joys and struggles. It can be overwhelming at times, but it is also one of the most rewarding experiences one can have. As parents, it is important to remember that you are not alone in this journey. There is support available to help you navigate the ups and downs of raising children. It is crucial to surround yourself with a strong support system that includes family, friends, and professionals who can offer guidance and reassurance when you need it.

One of the most important things to remember as a parent is to be kind to yourself. It is easy to get caught up in feelings of doubt and worry about whether you are doing a good job or if you are making the right decisions for your child. However, it is important to remember that no one is perfect, and there is no one-size-fits-all approach to parenting. Every child is unique, and what works for one family may not work for another. It is okay to make mistakes and to ask for help when you need it. Remember that you are doing the best you can, and that is all that matters.

Another key aspect of effective parenting is communication. It is important to establish open and honest communication with your children from a young age. Encourage them to express their thoughts and feelings, and listen attentively to what they have to say. This will help strengthen your relationship with your child and build trust between you. Communication is also essential when it comes to setting boundaries and expectations for your children. Being clear and consistent with your rules and consequences will help your child understand what is expected of them and will help prevent misunderstandings and conflicts.

As parents, it is important to also prioritize self-care. Taking care of yourself is not selfish, it is necessary in order to be the best parent you can be. Make time for activities that bring you joy and help you relax, whether it is exercise, reading, or spending time with friends. It is important to recharge your batteries and take care of your physical and mental health so that you can be present and engaged with your children. Remember that you cannot pour from an empty cup, so it is important to take care of yourself in order to take care of your family.

Lastly, remember to celebrate the small victories as a parent. Parenting is a tough job, and it is important to acknowledge and celebrate the progress you make with your children. Whether it is a successful potty training session, a good report card, or a peaceful family dinner, take the time to recognize your accomplishments, no matter how small they may seem. Celebrating these moments will help boost your confidence as a parent and reinforce the positive impact you have on your children's lives. Remember that you are not alone in this journey, and there is support available to help you navigate the highs and lows of raising children. Be kind to yourself, communicate openly with your children, prioritize self-care, and celebrate the small victories along the way. By following these principles, you can become the best parent you can be and create a loving and nurturing environment for your children to thrive in.

- Resources for further support

Having access to resources for further support can greatly enhance one's ability to succeed in various academic and professional pursuits. Whether you are a student seeking assistance with your coursework or a professional looking to develop new skills, having access to the right resources can make a significant difference in your success. In this article, we will explore some of the key resources available for further support and how you can effectively utilize them to achieve your goals.

One of the most valuable resources for further support is academic libraries. Libraries are not just a place to borrow books; they also provide access to a wealth of digital resources, including online journals, databases, and research guides. Many libraries also offer workshops and training sessions on topics such as research methods, citation styles, and information literacy. By taking advantage of these resources, you can enhance your research skills, find relevant sources for your assignments, and stay up-to-date on the latest developments in your field.

Another important resource for further support is academic tutoring services. Many universities and colleges offer tutoring services where students can receive one-on-one assistance with their coursework. Tutors can help clarify complex concepts, provide feedback on assignments, and offer study tips and strategies. Additionally, tutoring services can be a valuable resource for students who are struggling with specific subjects or who need additional help to reach their academic goals. By utilizing tutoring services, you can improve your understanding of course material and boost your academic performance.

Online learning platforms are also a valuable resource for further support. Platforms such as Coursera, Udemy, and Khan Academy offer a wide range of courses and tutorials on a variety of subjects, from computer programming to personal finance. These platforms allow you to learn at your own pace, access high-quality content from experts in the field, and connect with other learners through online forums and discussion boards. Whether you are looking to develop new skills, explore a new subject, or prepare for a certification exam, online learning platforms can be a valuable resource for further support.

Professional organizations are another valuable resource for further support, especially for individuals looking to advance their careers or build professional networks. Many professional organizations offer resources such as webinars, workshops, and networking events that can help you stay current in your field, connect with other professionals, and access job opportunities. By joining a professional organization related to your field, you can enhance your professional development, expand your knowledge base, and make valuable connections that can help you advance your career.

To summarize, mentorship can be a powerful resource for further support in both academic and professional settings. Having a mentor can provide you with guidance, feedback, and support as you navigate your academic or professional journey. A mentor can offer valuable insights based on their own experiences, help you set goals and develop a plan to achieve them, and provide a sounding board for your ideas and concerns. By seeking out a mentor who shares your interests and goals, you can leverage their expertise and support to help you succeed in your academic and professional endeavors. Whether you utilize academic libraries, tutoring services, online learning platforms, professional organizations, or mentorship, there are a variety of resources available to support you in your journey. By taking advantage of these resources and actively engaging with them, you can enhance your skills, expand your knowledge, and make valuable connections that can help you succeed. Remember, no matter where you are in your academic or professional journey, there are resources available to support you every step of the way.